Security and Privacy on Your PC

Manon Cassade

An imprint of PEARSON EDUCATION

PEARSON EDUCATION LIMITED

Head Office:
Edinburgh Gate
Harlow
Essex CM20 2JE
Tel: +44 (0) 1279 623623
Fax: +44 (0) 1279 431059

London Office:
128 Long Acre
London WC2E 9AN
Tel: +44 (0) 171 447 2000
Fax: +44 (0) 171 240 5771

⎯⎯⎯⎯⎯⎯

First published in Great Britain 2000

© Pearson Education Limited 2000

First published in 1999 as
Se Former En Un Jour: Partager le même PC
by CampusPress France
19, rue Michel Le Comte
75003 Paris
France

Library of Congress Cataloging in Publication Data
Available from the publisher.

British Library Cataloguing in Publication Data
A CIP catalogue record for this book can be obtained from the British Library.

ISBN 0-13-025781-8

10   9   8   7   6   5   4   3   2   1

Translated and typeset by Cybertechnics, Sheffield.
Printed and bound in Great Britain by Ashford Colour Press, Gosport, Hampshire.

The publishers' policy is to use paper manufactured from sustainable forests.

Contents

Introduction

Times are hard :-) You just cannot use your computer in peace any more, there is always someone else trumpeting that they have a right to use it too. Just a few years ago, the head of the family could use their machine without their partner and offspring claiming that they too have a right to use it. Times have changed; as of now, everybody wants to use it, because, what with the Web, discussion groups, better and better software, and so on, everyone has a use for it. Moreover, with some companies not being able to provide a PC for each user, you might have to share your computer with one or more colleagues. Next, let's talk about security and protection, which are neither vain words nor vain hopes: from now on, you can protect your computer from virus attacks, data loss and intrusion into your system via the Internet.

We have designed this book to teach you how to set up your computer in the best way so that sharing it and protecting it do not pose any problems. Here you will find absolutely everything about the steps to take in order to be able to share your PC in complete security and protect it from all possible and imaginable attacks. Fortified by this advice, you will be able to work in complete security and let your colleagues, children or partner have access to your PC without any worries.

■ Organisation of this book

This book has been organised in four different parts, each covering a particular topic; you will quickly be able to locate the topics which are of interest to you.

The first part looks at everything involved in sharing a PC; it contains four chapters, set out as follows:

- **Chapter 1** shows you how to create user profiles; this means configuring the PC differently for each user.
- **Chapter 2** shows you how to personalise Windows for each user.
- **Chapter 3** shows you how to personalise your use of the different browsers to fine tune your preferences for surfing the Internet.
- **Chapter 4** is devoted to electronic mail. You will find there all the tips and tricks needed for personalising your e-mail, creating multiple addresses, and so on.

The second part deals with everything to do with confidentiality; it contains two chapters, set out as follows:

- **Chapter 5** will teach you how to protect your data to ensure confidentiality.
- **Chapter 6** shows you how to surf the Internet, send electronic messages, and so on in complete confidentiality.

The third part deals with everything to do with protecting your PC; it contains five chapters, set out as follows:

- **Chapter 7** will teach you how to protect your system.
- **Chapter 8** explains how to protect your computer's data.
- **Chapter 9** shows you how to protect yourself from the Internet, that is blocking cookies, ActiveX and other Java which have the annoying tendency of destabilising the organisation of your data, and, in certain cases, prying into your system.

- **Chapter 10** reveals all about viruses, what they can do and how to protect yourself.

- **Chapter 11** gives you the low-down on the 'dangers' of the Internet and indicates procedures for protecting children when they are surfing the net. Next, you will see how to protect your computer from your little menaces and how to prevent them from making a complete shambles of your files and folders.

The fourth part analyses everything to do with passwords; it consists of one chapter, set out as follows:

- **Chapter 12** is devoted to the concept of the password, absolutely essential in the context of sharing and protecting a PC. You will find advice and tips for sensibly creating your password, protecting it, managing it, and so on.

■ Protection and confidentiality programs

In the coming weeks we are planning to publish a book which will be completely devoted to the various shareware and freeware programs which allow you to ensure complete protection and confidentiality when surfing the Internet. Indeed, a great many programs are being devoted to this kind of problem. Certain of them are referred to in this book. You will find below a list (not exhaustive) of programs with which to protect your surfing and ensure confidentiality of your data in the context of the Internet. All you have to do is visit the site indicated to download these products.

Programs to ensure the confidentiality of your browsing and the security of your PC:

- **I-SeeU** is a program which acts as a surveillance camera for your PC. You can download a demo version at the page **www.faxtastic.com/i-seeu.htm**.

- **ESafe Protect** is in fact a security pack for protecting your PC (configuring for multi-users, antivirus, Web filters, and so on). This program has to be bought. Refer to a computer magazine for details.
- **PGP** lets you encrypt your messages to protect their confidentiality. You can download a demo version from **www.pgpi.com**.
- **Cookie pal** is a program to protect against cookies. You can download this shareware from **www.kbura.com**.

■ Special symbols

As well as the text and illustrations in this book, you will find boxes which underline certain individual points.

 These boxes contain definitions, technical details or other information useful in connection with the subject matter.

 These boxes warn you about problems which might arise in certain circumstances. They also warn you what not to do. If you follow the instructions, you should not have any problems.

 These boxes give you tips or shortcuts (for example, key combinations) for carrying out certain tasks more easily or more speedily.

Part

'Every man for himself' or sharing a PC

■ ■

The first four chapters of this book are devoted to sharing a PC. When several of you work on a single PC, it is essential that each of you are able to personalise your work environment without altering that of the other users. For this purpose, Windows offers user profiles, as you will see during the first chapter. Thanks to user profiles, when Windows loads, all you have to do is type in the name of your user profile and within a few seconds you will retrieve the whole of your personal settings. Next, you will see how to personalise the desktop and the Internet connection settings, create personalised bookmarks, and so on.

To conclude, you will see how to set up personal e-mail accounts, use multiple addresses, and so on.

1

Each to their own user profile

■ ■

Basic principles
Creating user profiles
Administration of user profiles
Personalising user profiles

Sharing your PC with other people implies that you are forbidding or authorising other users to have access to your data, which is not always a simple matter. For this kind of problem, just using a password is obsolete. Windows 95 and 98 therefore offer you a means of precisely defining your own ideas about sharing; however, the first version of Windows 95, without the addition of Internet Explorer, offers only very limited possibilities, whereas Windows 98 is more powerful. The procedure for creating user profiles consists of defining a different user profile name for each person who uses the computer. This name is entered at boot up and allows the owner of the user profile to have access to the data, programs and files which they have a right to use. This implies also being able save in a log, for each user, all the activities engaged in. Each user profile has its own password, which works as an 'open sesame'. This procedure corresponds to the user profile that you are going to study throughout this chapter.

■ Basic principles

As long as you are the only person to use your computer, the steps to take to protect your work are relatively simple. To get to know them, you must refer to the second part of this book. On the other hand, as soon as there are several of you using the same computer, things get more complicated. Contrary to what you might think, it is not only business users who are affected by this problem: you may be a home user, but do your partner or children never use the computer? Are you sure that, at some time or other, there is not a risk of one of them accidentally deleting one of your files or even opening and changing them? User profiles are therefore the perfect solution for avoiding any problem of interference with your data.

How does it work?

When you create your user profile, you use a Wizard to define all the settings. In this way you can personalise the environment of your desktop, protect your confidential data, and so on. Once the different user profiles have been clearly defined, you access your user profile by opening the work session with the name of your user profile and the appropriate password. Windows then takes care of activating the settings and the Desktop configuration in the way that you defined earlier.

Level of real protection

We cannot conceal the fact that the user profiles in Windows 95 and 98 do not offer the same level of protection as operating systems such as Unix or Windows NT. However, they nevertheless allow you to protect your computer from clumsy handling and they make it noticeably more difficult for the comedians who would like to go rummaging in your confidential data.

■ Creating user profiles

Now you are going to go straight to the heart of the matter by studying the procedures for creating one or more user profiles, defining the settings, and so on.

Authorising multiple users

By default, the computer does not let you create user profiles. To create them, you therefore have to activate this option.

 All the procedures to do with user profiles (creation, editing, and so on) require you to restart the computer for the new settings to be activated.

To activate authorisation of multi-user use:

1. Click on **Start, Settings, Control Panel** (see Figure 1.1). Double-click on **Passwords**.

Figure 1.1 The Passwords module is accessible from the Control Panel.

2. Click on the **User Profiles** tab (see Figure 1.2).

3. Click on the **Users can customise their preferences...** option.

4. The user profile settings area is activated. It offers the following two options:

   ▪ **Include desktop icons and Network Neighborhood contents...** lets you record, for each user, the personalised settings of the interface and of the possible network resources.

   ▪ **Include Start menu and Program groups...** lets you personalise the Start menu and the program groups.

5. Click on **OK** to confirm.

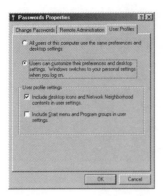

Figure 1.2 Activate the option to allow the creation of user profiles with the User tab.

Creating a user profile

Now that you have instructed Windows that it must allow the creation of user profiles, you have to create the user profile of the main PC user; this is the notion of Supervisor, that you will come across again in configuring Internet access. Of course, you need to have changed the different settings (Desktop, Start menu, and so on) for them to be recorded in the user profile. However, you can very well insert these changes after creating the user profile.

To create the first user profile:

1. Click on **Start, Settings, Control Panel** (see Figure 1.3). Double-click on **Users**.

2. Click on **New User**. Click on **Next**. Enter in the box the desired name for the user profile (see Figure 1.4). Click on **Next**.

3. Enter the desired password, then confirm it by entering it again in the box underneath. Click on **Next** (see Figure 1.5).

Figure 1.3 The Users module is accessible from the Control Panel.

Figure 1.4 Creating a user profile is done with the help of a Wizard.

4. Tick the items whose settings you wish to personalise in the context of your user profile (see Figure 1.6). Click on

Figure 1.5 The user profile is accessible by a password that you must not forget.

Next. Click on the option **Create new items...** to activate it. Click on **Next** and click on **Finish**. The new user profile is displayed in the list, click on **Close** and close the Control Panel.

Figure 1.6 Defining the items that you wish to personalise within your user profile.

 *All the elements that you tick will be empty if you activate the option **Create new elements**.*

Creating several user profiles

You have now created the first user profile. Next you need to suggest to your other colleagues (or your partner, your children, and so on) that they create their own user profiles.

To create other user profiles, click on **Start, Settings, Control Panel**. Double-click on **Users**. The user profile already created appears in the list (see Figure 1.7). Click on **New User**. Click on **Next,** then repeat the procedures as above: name the user profile, password, settings, and so on.

Figure 1.7 The list of user profiles created is displayed in the User Settings box.

Choice of user profile

Once some user profiles have been created, you can use them as soon as it becomes necessary. You can, for instance, choose to create a user profile which will contain all your confidential data. In this way, you will be able to work on the current documents using a certain user profile or without any user profile at all, and use another user profile for confidential documents.

To choose a user profile, when Windows has started, two configurations are possible:

- Either it is the User profile box which is displayed (see Figure 1.8), and you have to click on the desired user profile to activate it and click on **OK** to confirm.

Figure 1.8: Choose the user profile in the box which is displayed when Windows starts.

- Or it is the Password box which is displayed (see Figure 1.9), with the name of the last user profile that was used. All you have to do is enter the password, if this is the user profile that you wish to activate, or enter the name of the user profile and its password, then click on **OK**.

Figure 1.9 Enter the name of the user profile in the box which is displayed when Windows starts.

If you wish to work without using any user profile, hit the Esc key when the user profile box or password box is displayed.

Changing the user profile

Still in the context of working with several users, you have to be able to change user profiles quickly, to move from one user profile to another without too many complications.

To shut down a user profile, click on **Start, Log Off,** followed by the name of the active user profile (see Figure 1.10). In the dialog box which is displayed, click on **Yes** to confirm the shut down. In the new box which is displayed, select the new user profile to activate, as indicated in the procedures under the heading Choice of user profile.

Figure 1.10 The name of the active user profile is displayed opposite the Log Off command.

■ Administration of user profiles

Once you have created some user profiles, they will be accessible by selecting them and then entering the appropriate password. However, you will probably need to delete a user profile, edit it, and so on.

Deleting a user profile

To delete a user profile:

1. Click on **Start, Settings, Control Panel.** Double-click on **Users.**

Figure 1.11 The different user profiles created are displayed in the dialog box.

2. Click on the name of the user to be deleted. Click on **Delete** (see Figure 1.11). A confirmation dialog box is displayed (see Figure 1.12). Click on **Yes**.

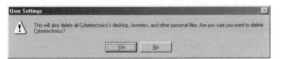

Figure 1.12 Confirming the deletion of the user profile.

3. Windows deletes the settings of the user profile. Click on **Close**. Then close the Control Panel.

Changing the password for a user profile

You notice that someone has used your user profile without your authorisation. So he must have found out your password! To prevent him trespassing again, you have to change the password.

To change the password of a user profile:

1. Click on **Start, Settings, Control Panel**. Double-click on the **Users** icon.
2. Click on the user profile whose password you wish to change. Click on **Choose a password** (see Figure 1.13).

Figure 1.13 Choosing a password for a user profile.

3. Enter the old password. Press the **Tab** key. Enter the new password, confirm it by entering it once more in the box below, and confirm by clicking on **OK**. Click on **Close**. Close the Control Panel.

Changing the settings of a user profile

You can easily change your settings:

1. Click on **Start, Settings, Control Panel**. Double-click on the **Users** icon.
2. Click on the user profile whose settings you wish to change. Click on **Change Settings** (see Figure 1.14). Deactivate the settings you no longer want and activate the settings of your choice. Click on **OK** to confirm. Click on **Close**, and close the Control Panel.

Copying the settings of a user profile

You barely have enough time to configure your own user settings, because you have so much work to do. One of your close colleagues (or your son!) has already spent a lot of time setting up a 'top level' user profile. You can ask him if you can copy his user profile and then alter it to suit yourself.

To copy a user profile:

Figure 1.14 The active settings are displayed. You can deactivate or activate them.

1. Click on **Start, Settings, Control Panel.** Double-click on the **Users** icon.

2. Click on the user profile whose settings you wish to copy. Click on **Make a copy.** The Wizard is displayed (see Figure 1.15), repeat the procedures already indicated under the heading Creating a user profile. Do not change the settings options when you are copying it! When you have finished, click on **Finish.** Click on **Close** and close the Control Panel.

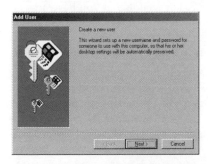

Figure 1.15 To copy a user profile, you use the same Wizard as for creating a user profile. Follow the procedures to copy the user profile selected.

■ Personalising user profiles

You will see in the third and fourth chapters how to protect or hide files, folders, programs, and so on, in the context of user profiles. For the time being, you are going to see what it is that each setting in the creation of a user profile allows you to personalise.

The first of the procedures to follow is to allow changes to the Start menu and the Desktop when you authorise the creation of user profiles (Refer to the heading Authorising multiple users).

Next, you need to choose certain options when you create or change a user profile as indicated below:

- **Create copies of the current items and their contents** lets you record, in the user profile, the active settings of the items you have chosen to activate (Start menu, Desktop, Documents menu, and so on). Thus, if the Start menu includes access to Chapter 2 of your forthcoming novel, this will be listed in the **Start** menu of the user profile.

- **Create new items to save disk space** lets you suggest, in the user profile, virgin (empty) items according to what you have chosen to activate. For example, if you have activated the item **Start** menu and you choose the option **Create new...**, the **Start** menu will be empty when you use this user profile (see Figure 1.16).

- **The Desktop folder and the Documents menu** handle the configuration of the Desktop (icons, programs, and so on) as well as the contents of the Documents menu.

 The Documents menu is accessible from the Start menu. It contains the latest files on which you have been working.

- **The Start** menu contains all the programs installed on the computer.

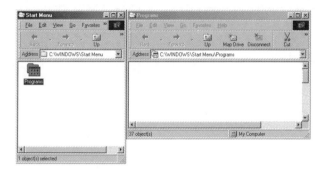

Figure 1.16 Empty Start menu.

- **The Favourites** folder contains all the Web addresses, files, folders, and so on, that you have placed there, as well as the active folders which appear there by default: channels, links and software updates.

- **Downloaded Web pages** contains exactly what its name describes.

- The **My Documents** folder contains everything that you have saved there in the course of your work sessions.

It is important to understand that all the changes made during the time that this user profile was being used (icon, program, files, and so on) will be active during the next session under this user profile.

2 Each to their own Windows

Once you have created your user profile, there are many ways in which you can personalise the configuration of the Desktop, Start menu, icons, and so on. In this chapter, you will find out about all the settings that Windows lets you customise and you will become the happy owner of Windows arranged to suit just you.

For all the procedures of this chapter to be activated in your user profile, you must define them after activating your user profile.

■ A Desktop to your liking

After the start of Windows, the first item that appears is the Desktop. The principle of it is not very hard to grasp: when you work at home, or in a professional environment, you have at your disposal a certain quantity of tools and 'furniture' to enable you to get organised and work at your best. You have a desk on which you place a calculator, pencils, diary and paper, cupboards in which you arrange your folders, and a basket in which to throw your waste paper, and so on. The principle of the Windows Desktop is the same. Each of its items constitutes one of your tools of work: for example, My Computer lets you quickly see the contents of your hard disk(s), the Recycle Bin is for getting rid of what you don't want, and so on. Each of the items is represented on the Desktop by an icon.

Personalising the Desktop Background

By default, the Desktop displays a not very attractive green background. You can change this, as well as the shape of the mouse pointer. Several solutions are available to you, which you will find detailed below.

In order to choose another background, right-click on the Desktop and select **Properties**. Click on the background tab (see Figure 2.1). In the Wallpaper box, a list of choices is displayed. Click on the various choices to view them in the picture symbolising the screen. Once you have made your selection, click on **OK** to confirm.

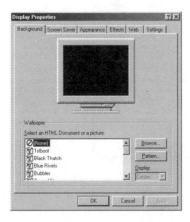

Figure 2.1 Windows offers several Backgrounds for the Desktop.

In order to choose a theme for Windows:

1. Click on **Start, Settings, Control Panel**. Double-click on **Desktop Themes** (see Figure 2.2).

   The active theme is displayed in the central panel of the dialog box.

2. Click on the arrow of the option **Theme** and select the required theme. In the right-hand column, you can activate the items that you wish to change, according to the theme chosen (icons, mouse pointers, screen saver, and so on).

3. In order to choose the pointers and the sounds that you wish to activate, click on **Pointers, Sounds, etc...** in the top right of the dialog box (see Figure 2.3), click on the type of mouse pointer desired, then click on **Close**. Click on **OK** to confirm it in the Desktop Themes dialog box.

Figure 2.2 Desktop themes let you speedily personalise all the items of the Desktop.

Figure 2.3 You can choose the types of pointers that you wish to activate.

If the pictures on offer do not suit you, you can perfectly well save onto your hard disk a picture that you particularly like or else browse on the Web in search of a background.

In order to display a background saved on the hard disk, right-click on the Desktop and select **Properties**. In the Background tab, click on **Browse**. In the dialog box which is displayed (see Figure 2.4), select the file desired and click on **Open**. The file containing the desired background is displayed in the list of choices. Click on the one you like in the list to select it, then click on **OK** in the Display Properties dialog box.

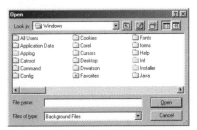

Figure 2.4 Save on your hard disk a picture for the background of your Desktop.

Quick reorganisation of the Desktop

It has to be admitted, we aren't all whizzes at organising, and, if you are anything like us, one day you will certainly find yourself with a real mess on your Desktop.

For your Desktop to be impeccably tidy when you come out of your user profile, right-click on the Desktop and select **Arrange Icons, Auto Arrange**.

Personalised icons on the Desktop

The icons on Desktop are not permanent, you can quickly choose other designs to personalise them and give them the form that you like.

In order to change the Desktop icons, right-click on the Desktop and select **Properties**. Click on the **Effects** tab. In the

Desktop Icons panel, you can see the different active icons. Click on the one that you wish to change, then click on **Change Icon** (see Figure 2.5). In the Change Icon dialog box, click on the design that suits you and click on **OK** to confirm. Use this procedure for all the icons that you wish to change. Click on **OK** to confirm in the Display Properties dialog box.

Figure 2.5 Choose the icons for the Desktop.

 *In order to retrieve speedily the default icons, right-click on the Desktop and click on the **Effects** tab. Click on **Default Icon**. Click on **OK** to confirm.*

■ Personalising the management of programs

By default, you access your programs by clicking on **Start, Programs,** then by selecting a program in the sub-menu which is displayed. It has to be admitted that these procedures are a bit tiresome. If you regularly use one or more programs, you can choose to display them as icons on the Desktop; you can also create a group of programs that you use in a precise work context, or even define the way the window of each program opens. You will find all these procedures and many others under this heading.

*You can open the contents of the **Start** menu without clicking, all you have to do is press the Windows key on your keyboard.*

Defining the size of a program's window

It is often tiresome to have to resize a window every time you open a program. Here is the procedure to follow so that the program is displayed automatically in the size of window desired.

In order to define the way an application's window opens, right-click on **Start** and select **Explore**. In Explorer, right-click on the program and select **Properties** (see Figure 2.6). If need be, click on the **Shortcut** tab. Click on the arrow of the **Run** option, then select the size of your choice (Normal, Minimize or Maximize). Click on **OK** to confirm.

Figure 2.6 Define the size of the window of the application when it is opened.

 The Normal or Maximize options correspond to full, whereas the Minimize option displays the program in the form of a button in the Taskbar.

Quick launch of programs

If you work almost all the time with the same applications, why not ask Windows to launch these automatically at the time you choose a user profile? Then you will no longer have to call up the applications one after the other. The solution lies therefore in placing shortcuts of these programs in the Start folder which contains all the applications and tools started automatically when Windows is launched.

In order to insert application shortcuts in the Start folder, right-click on **Start** and select **Explore**. In Explorer, double-click on **Windows** and click on **Start Menu**. The contents of the Start group are displayed (see Figure 2.7). In the right panel of Explorer, select the application desired, then, with the right mouse button, drag it into the Start folder. In the menu which is displayed, select **Create shortcut(s) here**. The shortcut of the application is displayed in the Start group. From now on, the application for which you have created a shortcut will be automatically launched at the same time as you choose a user profile.

Adding a program to the Start menu

By default, your programs are listed in the Programs command in the Start menu, which implies that you have to open the Start menu, select the command Programs, then select the program desired in a list. As long as you have only installed a few programs, this procedure will be relatively quick, but as soon as you have a lot of software... The solution therefore is to place your favourite programs directly in the Start menu.

In order to display programs in the Start menu:

1. Click with the right mouse button on **Start**, select **Explore**. In Explorer, look for the programs that you wish to display in the Start menu.

Figure 2.7 Creating a shortcut in the Start group.

2. Click on the icon of the desired program then, keeping the button pressed, drag it into **Start** in the Taskbar. Release it.

The program is displayed in the Start menu (see Figure 2.8).

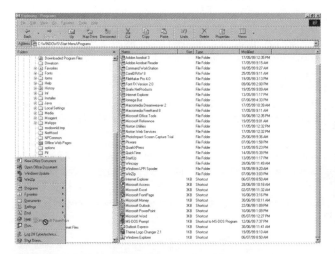

Figure 2.8 Add a program to the Start menu to access it there more speedily.

In order to delete an application from the Start group, click on **Start**, **Find**, **Files** *or* **Folders**. *Enter* **Start** *in the Name box. Press* **Enter**. *Double-click on* **Start** *in the list of the results of the search which is displayed. Click on the application to be delet-ed and press* **Delete**. *Confirm the deletion by clicking on* **Yes**. *Close the search window.*

Shortcut icons for programs

There is an even quicker method for launching programs: creating shortcut icons, displayed on the Desktop, for all the programs that you use frequently.

In order to create a shortcut icon for a program:

1. Click on **Start, Programs**.
2. In the sub-menu, right-click on the program for which you wish to create a shortcut icon, and drag it onto the Desktop holding down the mouse button. Let go. When the further menu is displayed (see Figure 2.9), select **Create shortcut(s) here**. The program shortcut icon is displayed on the Desktop.

Here is how to differentiate quickly between a shortcut icon and a program icon: a shortcut icon always has a small white arrow.

In order to delete a program shortcut, click on it to select it, then press **Delete**. *Confirm the deletion by clicking on* **Yes**.

You can choose to display large or small icons on the Desktop.

In order to change the size of the icons, right-click on the Desktop, and select **Properties**. Click on the **Effects** tab. Tick the option **Use large icons** to activate it (see Figure 2.10) and click on **OK** to confirm.

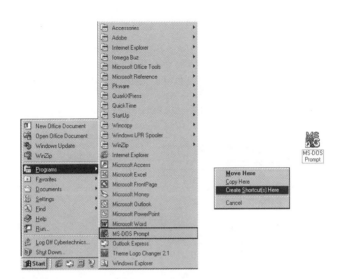

Figure 2.9 Create a shortcut icon for your favourite program.

Figure 2.10 Choose the display size of your icons.

....

You can also define precisely the size of your icons. Here is the procedure to follow.

In order to define precisely the size of the icons, right-click on the Desktop and select **Properties**. Click on the **Appearance** tab (see Figure 2.11). Click on the item arrow and select **Icons**. In the **Size** area, define the exact size in which you wish to display your icons. Click on **OK** to confirm.

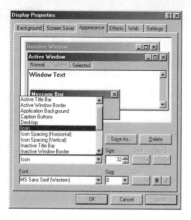

Figure 2.11 Define precisely the size of your icons.

Keyboard shortcuts faster than icons

In order to open a program, you have to open the Start menu, select the command Programs, then select the program in the submenu which is displayed. You have probably created some shortcut icons on the Desktop for faster access to the programs. But there is a snag: if you are working in some program or other and you cannot see the Desktop, you have to use the classic method, which is a bit long. The solution lies in the creation of a keyboard shortcut for opening a program.

In order to create a keyboard shortcut for a program:

1. Click with the right mouse button on **Start** and select **Find**. In the name box, enter *programname.lnk* and press **Enter**.

   The result of the search is displayed at the bottom of the dialog box.

2. Click with the right mouse button on the program icon and select **Properties**. Click on the **Shortcut** tab (see Figure 2.12). In the Shortcut Key box, which for the moment displays None, press on the key (or keys) that you wish to use to invoke your program speedily, for example Shift+A. Click on **OK** to confirm. Close the Find dialog box.

Figure 2.12 Create a keyboard shortcut for launching a program.

From now on, you just have to press this keyboard shortcut to launch the program.

■ Accessibility

Windows offers several ways to optimise its interface and thus let anyone personalise the use of operating system. The accessibility options are one of the strong points of these personalisations. In fact, all of these options let you set up the system according to your wishes and above all according to possible problems of hearing, sight, and so on.

*All the accessibility options are themselves accessible from the Control Panel by double clicking on **Accessibility**.*

Gagging Windows

By default, Windows assigns a certain number of sounds to certain events. If you are one of those who hates on-board computers and other machines that speak, you can choose to gag Windows and prevent it from making any sound at all.

In order to delete the association of sounds with certain events:

1. Click on **Start, Settings, Control Panel**. Double-click on **Sounds** (see Figure 2.13).

2. Click on the arrow of the option **Schemes** and select **No Sounds**. Click on **OK** to confirm.

Viewing the movements of the mouse

When you work in a program such as Publisher or any other program that needs precision in the movements of the mouse, it is essential that these movements be very easy to view. When you begin to use Windows, it isn't very simple to see the movements of the mouse on the screen. On a portable, however, the mouse pointer frequently disappears altogether with no trace of the trackball. Windows offers a solution which is just the job for this problem: displaying mouse trails: as soon as the mouse moves, a trail appears on screen.

Figure 2.13 Possible deletion of the sounds assigned to certain events in Windows.

To display the mouse trails:

1. Click on **Start, Settings, Control Panel**. Double-click on Mouse. Click on the **Motion** tab (see Figure 2.14).

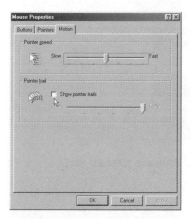

Figure 2.14 Movement of the mouse pointer.

2. Tick on the option **Show pointer trails** to activate it. Define the size of the trail by sliding the cursor along the scale located beneath the option. Click on **OK** to confirm.

From now on, each time you move your mouse on screen, you will see a succession of pointers appearing, showing the movement made.

The taming of the mouse

You can increase or reduce the speed of your mouse as well as its click speed. You can also tell Windows whether you are left or right handed.

In order to change the speed and the type of use of the mouse:

1. Click on **Start, Settings, Control Panel.** Double-click on **Mouse.** Click on **Buttons** (see Figure 2.15).

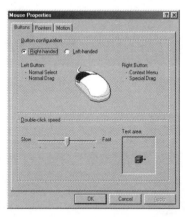

Figure 2.15 Define the settings of the mouse: speed and use.

2. In the Button configuration panel, tick on the option you want. In the double-click speed panel, drag the cursor to define the speed desired. Click on **OK** to confirm.

3 Each to their own Internet

Each to their own connection
Personalising your Browser

For all the procedures of this chapter to be activated in your user profile, you must define them after activating your user profile.

In the course of this chapter, you are going see how to define, for each user, an Internet connection, then you will study the different possibilities for personalising your browser: personalised bookmarks, personalised favourites, and so on.

■ Each to their own connection

When sharing your PC, it is essential for each user to have his own connection in order to avoid any confusion. In fact, if you each have a different Internet service provider (or a different connection), you avoid the risk of undeserved reproaches such as: 'You spent three hours on the Net', when in fact you only spent a few minutes. If you have opted for itemised billing, you will quickly be able to find out how much time each person has spent on line, and in this way share the costs equally.

Principles of Internet connection

As you already know, the Internet is the network of networks, that is, it lets computers all over the world communicate with each other. That being so, for this communication to work, it is essential to have, and install, a certain number of items.

Items needed for an Internet connection, in addition to a computer, obviously:

- Internal or external modem connecting the PC to the telephone line;
- Subscription to an Internet service provider.

Once you have these, you need to configure the PC in order to establish the connection. It is essential to understand 'how it works'. Let us compare it with the satellite reception on your television set: to be able to have access to the satellite channels, you must take out a subscription (corresponding to your ISP subscription), install an aerial (corresponding to the modem), have a decoder (corresponding to the browser) and a TV (corresponding to the computer). The satellite beams the data to the aerial, which sends it to the decoder, which retranslates the language and displays it on your television. As regards the Internet, the latter sends the data to the ISP who passes it on to your computer by means of the modem. The data is translated into images, texts, sounds, and so on, by the browser. It is as simple as that, in theory. A picture being worth a thousand words, refer to Figure 3.1, which clearly explains how the Internet works.

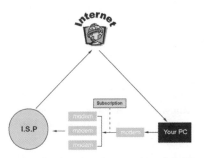

Figure 3.1 How the Internet connection works.

The above description is deliberately simplistic; in reality, it is a bit more complicated. In fact, so that the information passes between all the computers, it is essential to use a communication protocol common to all the linked computers. Without this protocol, there is no communication! On the Internet, it is the TCP/IP protocol which rules. On the other hand, for your modem to connect to your ISP, it is essential to use a connection protocol called PPP, as well as the dial-up number. You are going to see in the following sections how to put in place these different protocols. For now, acquaint yourself with the different connections and all the cards you will be using.

Configurations for the connection:

■ dial-up networking;

■ installation and configuration of TCP/IP protocol;

■ connection to the ISP.

 So that each of the users has his own personal connection, it is essential that each configuration be set up in a different user profile!

Installation of Dial-up Networking

First of all, you must activate dial-up networking, without which it is impossible for you to connect to an Internet service provider. This operation is a one-off, it will not be necessary to repeat it for each user profile.

In order to install dial-up networking:

1. Click on **Start, Settings, Control Panel**. Double-click on **Add/Remove programs**. Click on the **Windows Setup** tab (see Figure 3.2).

   Wait a few seconds for the list of components already installed to be displayed.

2. Click on **Communications** in the list of installed components. Click on **Details** (see Figure 3.3).

3. Click on the option **Dial-up Networking** in the list of components. Insert the Windows CD-ROM into the CD-ROM drive. Click on **OK** when the installation is finished.

4. Click on **OK** to close the dialog box Windows Setup dialog box. Close the panel.

Figure 3.2 Display the list of components already installed.

Figure 3.3 Install dial-up networking.

Creating connections to different ISPs

Now that you have installed the dial-up networking, you are going to be able to set up the connection to the Internet service provider of your choice. All the details that you are going to have to enter are given to you by the Internet service provider when you take out your subscription.

To create a connection to the ISP:

1. Activate your user profile (if necessary, restart). Click on **Start, Programs, Accessories, Communications**. In the sub-menu, click on **Dial-up Networking** (see Figure 3.4).

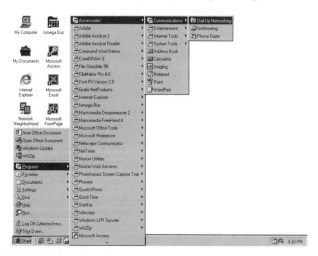

Figure 3.4 The Dial-up Networking window contains the different connections to ISPs.

2. Click on the icon **Make New Connection**.
3. The first stage of the Internet Connection Wizard is displayed (see Figure 3.5). Click on **Next**. In the second stage, enter a name (for example, the name of your user profile) in the option **Type a name...** then click on the arrow of the

option **Select a device** and select the name of your modem.
Click on **Next** (see Figure 3.6).

Figure 3.5 A Wizard helps you set up the connection.

Figure 3.6 Now you must enter the telephone number of the ISP.

4. Enter the area code as well as the telephone number of the
   ISP in the appropriate boxes. Click on **Next**. Click on
   Finish. Click with the right mouse button on the new connection icon and select **Properties**. In the dialog box which
   is displayed, type in if necessary the different settings for
   your connection (area code, telephone number, server
   type, and so on).

5. For a connection icon to be displayed on the Desktop of your user profile, right-click on the icon of your new connection and select **Create shortcut(s) here**. In the dialog box which is displayed, click on **Yes** to confirm.

The shortcut icon is displayed on the Desktop. All you have to do is double-click to launch the connection.

For the other users of the PC to create their own connections, all they have to do is repeat these steps, in their own user profile.

Installation of the TCP/IP protocols

You are reaching the final stage of configuring the connection between the computer and the Internet. Obviously, all the following procedures must take place in the context of your user profile, otherwise, you will not be able to make a connection! At the start of this chapter, you learned that it is the TCP/IP protocol which rules the Internet and ensures that data circulates between the computers on the network. All the information that you need to enter is supplied by your ISP.

When you are the only person to use the PC and, therefore, the Internet connection, the settings of the TCP/IP protocol are done through Network, accessible from the Control Panel. You have to activate the TCP/IP protocol, then define the properties. That changes when there are several of you using the same PC and different connections.

*If you encounter any problem in installing the TCP/IP protocol, double-click on **Network** in the Control Panel. If the TCP/IP protocol does not appear, click on **Clients for the Microsoft network** in the list and click on **Add**. Click on **Protocol** in the list and click on **Add**. Click on **Microsoft** in the list of manufacturers, then on TCP/IP in the list of network protocols. Click on **OK** to confirm. Click on **OK** in the Network dialog box. Close the Control Panel and restart.*

In order to install a TCP/IP protocol for your connection, right-click on your connection icon in the Dial-up networking window. Select **Properties**. Click on the **Server Types** tab (see Figure 3.7). In the Allowed network protocols box, click on the **TCP/IP** option. Click on **TCP/IP Settings** (see Figure 3.8). Activate the **Specify an IP address** option, then complete the IP address box. Activate the **Specify name server addresses...** option, then complete the different boxes Primary DNS, Secondary DNS, Primary WINS, and so on. Click on **OK** to confirm.

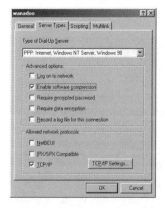

Figure 3.7 The Server types tab which lets you set up your personal TCP/IP protocol.

Each user just has to repeat these steps, within their own user profile

Finding out the costs of each user

There are various shareware utilities that let you work out, to the nearest penny, the cost of the Internet connection. The best known of these is TarifCom, a small program which is absolutely brilliant! Thanks to this program, you will be able

Figure 3.8 Complete the different boxes of your TCP/IP protocol.

to find out the length of time logged on to the Internet, and the cost, for each Internet user. No more working it all out on a pocket calculator: this program will do the 'dirty work' for you.

To download TarifCom, just launch any search engine and enter *Tarifcom* in the search field. A number of sites will be displayed, since this shareware is very well known. Choose a download site, then download the product. Install it in the usual way. Don't forget, if you decide to use it, to pay your small contribution to Philippe Supera, the inventor of this product. Once it is installed and each of you have done some browsing, double-click on the TarifCom icon which is displayed in the taskbar, next to the clock (see Figure 3.9).

The total amount of the connections is displayed. In order to see the details of each connection as well as the name of the user, click on the icon displaying an eye (see Figure 3.10). Everything is recorded, no-one can 'cheat' any more!

Figure 3.9 TarifCom lets you know the exact cost of connections to the Internet.

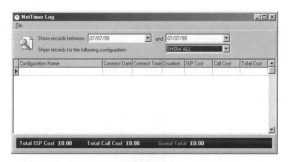

Figure 3.10 Find out the time and the amount of connections of each user.

■ Personalising your Browser

It is thanks to the browser that you are going to being able to decode HTML and thus view on your computer the pictures and text, and so on, available on the Web. It is also the browser that lets you send electronic messages, transfer files... Without it, it would be impossible to read or receive anything at all. There are two main browsers on the market: Netscape Communicator (Navigator module) and Internet Explorer. You will find in the following pages the options for personalising each of these browsers.

Of course, for any of the personalisation options to take effect, it is essential to have activated your user profile.

Personal profiles

You can define your user profile by indicating your identity, address, and so on. You will find below the procedures to follow for each browser.

For personal profiles in Internet Explorer:

1. Run Internet Explorer. Click on **View, Internet Options**. Click on the **Content** tab, then on **Edit the user profile** (see Figure 3.11).

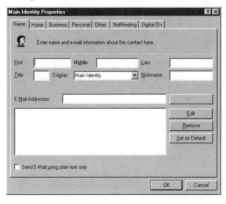

Figure 3.11 Define your user profile in Internet Explorer.

2. Move between the different tabs and fill in the boxes that apply to you. Click on **OK** to confirm. Click on **OK** in the Internet Options box.

For personal profiles in Navigator:

1. Run Netscape Communicator, click on **Communicator, Navigator**. Click on **Edit, Preferences**. Double-click on **Mail & Newsgroups** in the left panel. Click on **Identity** (see Figure 3.12).

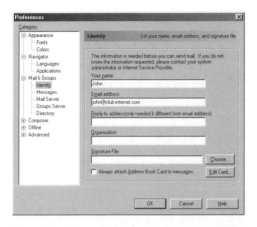

Figure 3.12 Define your user profile in Netscape Navigator.

2. Complete the different boxes in the right-hand panel. Click on **OK** to confirm.

Browsing options

The two main browsers offer too many options for us to be able to study them all here. We indicate below just the most important, in both browsers.

In order to define the options for browsing with Internet Explorer, click on **View, Internet Options** (see Figure 3.13). Move between the different tabs and choose your browsing options. Click on **OK** to confirm when you have finished.

In order to define the options for browsing in Netscape Communicator, click on **Edit, Preferences** (see Figure 3.14). Select the different options displayed in the left-hand panel of the dialog box and choose your browsing options. Click on **OK** to confirm when you have finished.

Figure 3.13 Main options for browsing with Internet Explorer.

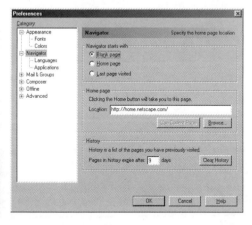

Figure 3.14 Main options for browsing in Netscape Communicator.

Personalised Bookmarks

Bookmarks are a feature of Netscape Communicator. They are comparable to the bookmarks that you place in a book when you want to be able to find a certain page quickly. You can therefore 'mark' Web pages and sites that you enjoy, and access them speedily by selecting the corresponding bookmark. Thus, when you work in your user profile, you have quick access to your favourite sites.

The first step is to create a folder containing your bookmarks. In order to do this, in Netscape Navigator, click on **Communicator, Bookmarks**. In the sub-menu, click on **Edit Bookmarks**. In the window which is displayed, click on **Edit, Bookmark Properties** (see Figure 3.15). Fill in the various boxes and click on **OK** to confirm.

Figure 3.15 Define the properties of your bookmarks.

In order to create a bookmark, right-click in the desired site or page, and select **Add bookmark** in the menu displayed. These procedures are to be done when you are online.

In order to view a bookmark, click on **Go** and select the bookmark desired. You can also **Go To bookmarks** and click on the one that interests you.

In order to delete or change a bookmark, open the bookmarks and make your changes.

Personalised favourites

In Internet Explorer, it is your favourites that act as bookmarks and which mark the pages which you particularly like.

In order to create a favourite, right-click in the site or the page being viewed, and select **Add to favourites** in the menu displayed. A dialog box is displayed, asking you to define how you wish to subscribe to this favourite (see note). Click on your choice, then click on **OK** to confirm. These procedures are to be done when you are online.

 As you already know, the Web is changing all the time. Hence, pages evolve at great speed. If you wish to keep abreast of any changes carried out at one of your favourite sites, you have to subscribe to it. Thus, each modification of the site will be echoed in your favourite, according to how you configured it (information by e-mail or directly on the Web).

In order to view a favourite, click on the **Favourites** icon. In the panel which is displayed, to the left-hand side of the screen, click on the favourite that you wish to view.

4 Each to their own electronic mail

Basic principles of electronic mail
Sharing the e-mail program
Personalising the e-mail program

In the course of this chapter we are going to tackle the subject of sharing electronic mail and newsgroups. You will be seeing how to set up multiple e-mail addresses on a single Internet connection and how to create multiple address books for your contacts, as well as looking at the various ways of personalising your e-mail program.

■ Basic principles of electronic mail

Before starting work on this, it is essential for you to understand how electronic mail works. As you probably know already, this is the oldest Internet service, and its use is also as widespread as the Web itself. It allows you to send messages anywhere in the world in record time and, above all, at very little cost. You can attach to your electronic mail text files, picture, sounds, and so on.

The principle is the same as for the posted letter: you write a message to a person then you 'post' it to their e-mail address. As soon as the addressee logs on to his e-mail system, he will receive your message. Just as with the Internet connection, the principle seems simple; however, behind this simplicity lies hidden a whole system of routing. Here in a few lines is exactly how it works. The moment you send your message, it is sent to your access provider with the SMTP protocol. The provider sends your message to the addressee's provider, who gets it to its 'client' using the POP protocol. That's why you have to indicate a server for incoming mail (POP) and a server for outgoing mail (SMTP) when you create your e-mail address.

The principal e-mail programs

Just as for browsers, there are two main e-mail programs: Messenger (see Figure 4.1), which is part of Netscape Communicator; and Outlook Express (see Figure 4.2), which is part of Internet Explorer. Of course there are many others, such as Eudora, Mosaic, and so on, but we cannot study them all here. All the procedures that you will discover in the course of this chapter will therefore only apply to the two main e-mail programs.

Netscape Communicator and Internet Explorer are given away for free. You can obtain them from the following two sites: netscape.com and microsoft.com. You can also download the latest available version by selecting the hypertext link Download offered systematically at these sites. And, if you do not yet have a browser, get hold of any computer magazine: most of them contain CD-ROMs for installing one of the main browsers.

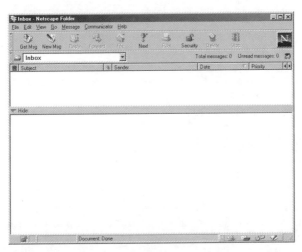

Figure 4.1 E-mail system of Netscape Communicator: Messenger.

*In order to launch Messenger, open Netscape Communicator then click on **Communicator**, **Messenger – In box**.*

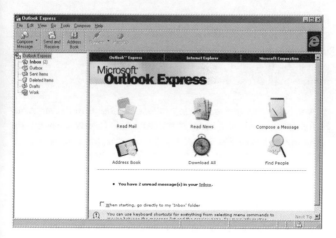

Figure 4.2 E-mail system of Internet Explorer: Outlook Express.

*In order to launch Outlook Express, click on the icon **Start Outlook Express** in the Quickstart bar or, in Internet Explorer, click on **Go to**, **Mail**.*

■ Sharing the e-mail program

It is important that each user has his own e-mail address as well as his own address book and distribution list. Do not worry about the cost of these multiple e-mail addresses: most good providers offer several e-mail addresses (up to five) for the same connection.

Creating multiple e-mail addresses in Outlook Express

If you cannot, for financial or other reasons, manage to have several providers, the solution is to install several e-mail addresses on a single connection. Thus, each user will be able to receive his mail at his own address, without the risk of cluttering up the mailboxes of the other users.

In Outlook Express, two solutions are offered. You will find them below. The details to enter are supplied by your service provider.

In order to create multiple e-mail addresses apart from the user profiles:

1. In Outlook Express, click on **Tools, Accounts**. Click on the **Mail** tab (see Figure 4.3). The main connection with the first e-mail address is displayed. Click on Add and select **Mail** in the menu. In the first stage of the Wizard, enter your name, then click on **Next**.

Figure 4.3 The Internet Account window lets you create new e-mail addresses.

2. In the new stage, enter the new e-mail address (see Figure 4.4). Click on **Next**. Enter the names of the SMTP and POP protocols (for example *mail.force9.net*). Click on **Next**. You now have to enter the account name as well as its password. Click on **Next**. If need be, enter the account name again and click on **Next**.

3. If need be, click on the option **Connection using a telephone line** and click on **Next**. Click on the scrolling list arrow and select the modem desired. Click on **Next** (see Figure 4.5). In the new stage, indicate if you are using the existing connection or another. Click on **Next**. Click on **Finish**. In the Mail tab, the two e-mail addresses are displayed, the new address displays the figure (1). Click on **Close**.

Figure 4.4 A Wizard helps you when you want to create your new e-mail addresses.

Figure 4.5 You need to tell the Wizard which connection you are going to use.

4. Repeat these procedures for each e-mail address.

From now on, to read the mail of the different addresses, click on the icon **Send and receive**. The connection is established and the mail is delivered to each address. All you have to do is read it!

In order to create a new e-mail address in a user profile:

1. Open your user profile. In Outlook Express, click on **Tools, Accounts**. An Internet connection wizard is displayed (see Figure 4.6). Repeat the procedures for creating a connection indicated in the course of the second chapter. When you have finished, click on Add and select **Mail** in the scrolling menu.

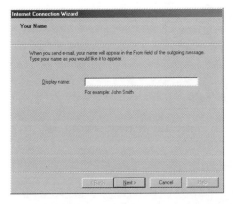

Figure 4.6 Use the Wizard to create the new connection.

2. Repeat all the procedures indicated under the previous heading.

In order to read your mail, all you have to do is open your user profile and launch Outlook Express. Next, click on the icon **Send and receive**. The connection is established and the mail is delivered to your e-mail address.

Creating several e-mail addresses in Messenger

Just as in Outlook Express, you can create several e-mail addresses for the same connection in Messenger. There is just one procedure, which is:

1. Click on Start in the Windows taskbar. Choose **Programs, Netscape Communicator, Utilities, User Profile Manager.**

Figure 4.7 The User Profile Manager lets you create several e-mail addresses for the same connection.

2. Click on **New**. Click on **Next** in the first stage. In the new stage, enter your name as well as the new e-mail address. Click on **Next**. Enter the name of the user profile and click on **Next** (see Figure 4.8). Now you have to enter your name, your e-mail address and the SMTP server. Click on **Next**. Enter again your name and the name of the POP server. Click on **Next**. Finally, you might indicate your News server and click on **Finish**.

   Netscape is launched automatically. Close it if you do not wish to use it immediately.

In order to read the mail at your e-mail address, you have to launch Netscape, then, in the window, double-click on **Utilities,** then on **User Profile Manager**. In the Manager, double-click on the appropriate user profile corresponding to your e-mail address. All you have to do now is read your mail.

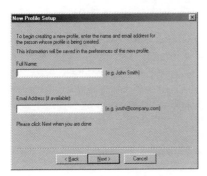

Figure 4.8 Fill in the various boxes before creating your new e-mail address.

Creating multiple address books in Outlook Express

Just like everyone else, when you wish to send a letter to one of your friends or relations, and so on, you refer to your address book to find out quickly the address of your addressee. In fact, we don't all have the memory of an elephant, and it is impossible for us to remember the addresses of all our correspondents! Conscious of this obvious fact, the creators of Microsoft have installed the address book tool to list your addressees along with their e-mail addresses, their Web addresses, their telephone numbers, and so on. In this way, you will not have to search feverishly for an address when you want to send a message.

The basic principles for creating an address book are simple: you open it and you create a new contact for each of your addressees. A file is created for each, all you have to do is fill it in. Consequently, you will just have to select the file to discover automatically the address of the addressee. By default, Outlook Express provides a single address book. If you share the PC with other users, you can of course use the same address book, but if you wish to preserve your privacy, the best solution is to create several address books.

In order to create multiple address books:

1. Open your user profile. In Outlook Express, click on **Address Book** from the Inbox folder (see Figure 4.9). In the address book, click on the **New contact** icon (see Figure 4.10).

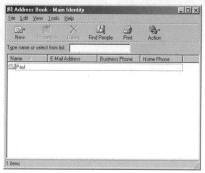

Figure 4.9 The address book will contain all the information on the people to whom you send electronic mail.

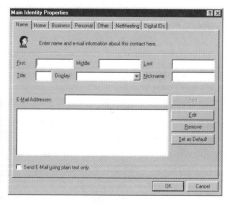

Figure 4.10 In order to create a new contact, you have to fill in the different boxes, in the different tabs.

2. Fill in the contact form. Move through all the tabs that you wish to fill in. Click on **OK** when you have finished. The new contact is displayed in the list in the address book. Repeat these procedures for all your contacts. Close the address book when you have finished.

Repeat these procedures for each address book, in the user profile of each user.

In order to use the address book, just activate your user profile and open the address book in Outlook Express.

Creating multiple address books in Messenger

It is pointless for us to go over again what we have just said about the address book in Messenger; indeed, the principle is the same as in Outlook Express. However, the procedures to follow may be different.

In order to create several personal address books in Messenger, create a user profile in Netscape if this has not already been done (to find out the procedures, refer to the heading Creating several addresses...). Once the user profile has been created, all you have to do is to activate it before launching Messenger. In the e-mail program, click on **Communicator, Address Book** (see Figure 4.11). Click on the **New card** icon (see Figure 4.12). In the form on the card, fill in the different desired options. Click on **OK** when you have finished. The new card is displayed in the list. Repeat these steps to create all the cards. Close the address book when you have filled in all the cards.

In order to use your personal address book, all you have to do is activate your user profile and open Messenger's address book.

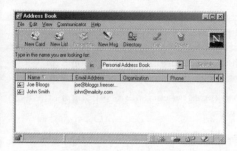

Figure 4.11 The address book will contain all the information about people to whom you send electronic mail.

Figure 4.12 In order to create a new card, you need to fill in the different options, in the different tabs.

▪ Personalising the e-mail program

There are many possible ways to personalise your e-mail program. We are going to point out a few of them. Remember to personalise the e-mail program without damaging the e-mail setup of anyone else; you need to set up all these personal features in the context of your user profile.

General personalising options

Most of the options for personalising your e-mail are accessible by a command in both programs.

In order to have access to the general personalisation options in Outlook Express, click on **Tools**, **Options** (see Figure 4.13). Move between the different tabs and activate, or deactivate, the desired options. Click on **OK** to confirm.

Figure 4.13 The Tools, Options command lets you have access to full range of options for personalising Outlook Express.

In order to have access to the general personalisation options in Messenger, click on **Edit**, **Preferences** (see Figure 4.14). In the left-hand panel, double-click on **Mail and News**, the contents are displayed below. Move between the contents and activate or deactivate the desired options. Click on **OK** to confirm.

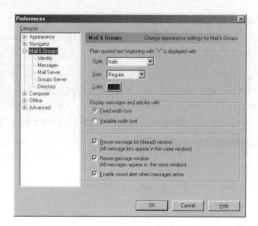

Figure 4.14 The Edit, Preferences command lets you have access to the full range of options for personalising Messenger.

Signing the mail

You can attach an electronic signature to your mail. Here is what to do in each e-mail program.

In order to attach a signature to all your Outlook Express messages, click on **Tools, Writing paper**. Click on **Signature** (see Figure 4.15). Enter your signature in the top panel. Define the desired options and click on **OK** to confirm. Click on **OK** in the dialog box Tools.

In order to attach a signature to all Messenger messages, first of all create it in a file and save it to your hard disk. Next, in Messenger, click on **Edit, Preferences**. Click on **Identity** in the right-hand panel (sub-menu of Mail and news) (see Figure 4.16). Click on **Select** in the **Signature file** option. Double-click on the file containing your signature. Click on **OK** to confirm.

Figure 4.15 Insert a signature in your messages created in Outlook Express.

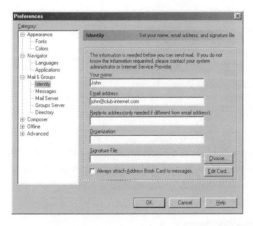

Figure 4.16 Insert a signature in your messages created in Messenger.

Creating folders

In order to classify your messages correctly, you can create personal folders in the e-mail program. As soon as you receive some messages, all you have to do is file them in the various folders. You will thus have a well-organised in-tray.

In order to create folders in Outlook Express, in your user profile, click on **File, New, New Folder** (see Figure 4.17). Enter the name of the new folder in the upper box, then click on the directory which is to contain it in the list below. Click on **OK** to confirm.

Figure 4.17 Create folders in Outlook Express.

In order to create folders in Messenger, in your user profile, click on **File, New folder** (see Figure 4.18). In the box which is displayed, enter the name of the folder, then indicate, in box beneath, in which directory you wish to place this folder. Click on **OK** to confirm.

Figure 4.18 Create folders in Messenger.

Choice of a background

In order to lend greater originality to your messages, you can choose to use stationery. Thus your messages will be like a traditional letter, but with greater speed.

In order to choose stationery in Outlook Express, in your user profile, click on the **New Message** icon (see Figure 4.19). Fill in the different boxes according to the traditional methods of creating a message. Click on **Format, Apply Stationery**. A list of choices is displayed. Click on the one that suits your needs. The background is displayed in the message, all you have to do is send it.

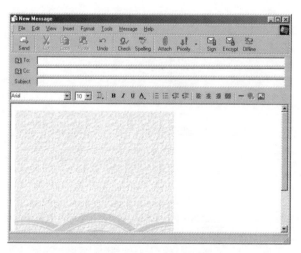

Figure 4.19 Choosing stationery in Outlook Express.

Part

II

Protecting your privacy

■ ■

If you have carefully studied the preceding chapters, you now know how to create user profiles, personalised bookmarks, personal e-mail accounts, and so on. However, there still remains a key factor to consider when sharing a PC: confidentiality. In fact, the user profiles let you define your own settings without actually preserving your privacy. You will see therefore, in the course of the next two chapters, how to keep your data, your browsing, your e-mail, and so on confidential.

5 Protecting your confidential data

Managing the deletion of items properly

Cover your tracks

Playing hide and seek with items

In the course of this chapter, you will see how to hide the data that must remain confidential. You will also study all the procedures to follow to prevent anyone from finding out about your latest piece of work or from altering any of your files. But, to begin with, you will see how to delete files permanently.

As with the previous chapters, the procedures forbidding items must be implemented in the context of your user profile.

■ Managing the deletion of items properly

In the beginning, the files deleted from a PC were deleted permanently; it was impossible to recover them. Later on, the designers of Windows, aware that human stupidity is infinite, installed a safeguard with the Recycle Bin. In fact, the Recycle Bin of Windows is exactly the same thing as the waste paper basket under your desk: everything you throw away in it is recoverable as long as you have not emptied it. Therefore, when you delete a file from Explorer, it is still recoverable from the Recycle Bin. Although this function is very useful, it can become dangerous: when, for instance, you throw away an extremely confidential file and forget to empty the Recycle Bin on your Desktop, anyone will be able to restore this file in its original folder and read it. Here are several procedures to avoid this kind of trouble.

The Recycle Bin only stores files discarded from the hard disk; files deleted from a floppy disk or network are permanently lost.

Doing without the Recycle Bin

If you are sure that you will never need to recover deleted files, the solution is to tell Windows that the items that you throw away must never be placed in the Recycle Bin.

In order never to use the Recycle Bin:

1. In the Desktop, right-click on the Recycle Bin icon and select **Properties** (see Figure 5.1).

Figure 5.1 Configure the Recycle Bin according to your wishes.

2. Tick the option **Do not move files to the Recycle Bin...** to activate this. Click on **OK** to confirm.

*If, just for once, you do not wish to use the Recycle Bin, all you have to do is to hold down the **Shift** key at the same time as the **Delete** key when you are deleting an item.*

Permanent deletion of files

The creators of Windows are kind to the absent-minded: the files deleted from the Recycle Bin are not, in fact, permanently destroyed. In fact, all you have to do is use a program such as Norton Utilities to recover data that you thought was lost forever. Nevertheless, this function becomes problematic when you wish to delete data permanently, since anyone knowing how to use a data-recovery utility will be able to recover your discarded files.

To enable you to understand the process of data recovery better, here is 'the low-down'. Hard disks are composed of numerous sectors each containing a quantity of data. Thus, a file that has been saved can be stored on several sectors. As soon as the hard disk begins filling up, the data is spread throughout the disk. In order to facilitate searching, the computer has a file allocation table (FAT); these allocation tables indicate, for each file, where and how the data is saved. When you erase a file, the computer erases all the information about the file in the allocation tables, the sectors used are therefore considered from then on as free, but, in fact, the data is not erased as long as the sectors have not been re-used. Thus, if someone explores the hard disk with a recovery utility, he will be able to recover the data marked "free" but not yet over-written.

This kind of problem can be got round thanks to tools called file crushers. With these, the files are permanently destroyed and irrecoverable, even by the most effective recovery tools. The use of these programs resembles normal deletion in every way: in the program, you select one or more files then delete it/them. File Shredder is the most popular file crusher, since it lets you select any file or folder, then delete it with a simple click.

In order to download File Shredder:

1. Launch your browser and go online. In the address bar, enter **www.lushanntechnologies.com** and press **Enter**. The site of Lushann Technologies is displayed (see Figure 5.2).
2. Click on the hypertext link **File Shredder.** In the new page of the site, go down the page, then click on **Download File Shredder.** A dialog box asking if you wish to download this shareware is displayed. If need be, tick on the option **Save to hard disk** and click on **OK** (see Figure 5.3).

Note carefully the name of the folder in which the shareware is going to be downloaded.

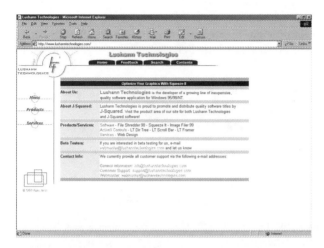

Figure 5.2 The site of Lushann Technologies offers several shareware programs, including File Shredder.

Figure 5.3 Download the shareware on to your hard disk.

3. After about twenty minutes, the shareware has downloaded to your hard disk. Click on **OK** in the dialog box. Disconnect and close your browser. Right click the mouse button on **Start** and select **Explore**. In Explorer, double-click on the file containing the download. Unzip FS98.

Once you have unzipped the download file, you obtain three different files. Now you need to proceed to installing the product (see Figure 5.4).

Figure 5.4 WinZip shows that File Shredder will contain three different files after decompression.

4. Double-click on **setup**. The installation starts; by default, the program is placed in the Program Files folder (see Figure 5.5). Follow the procedure.

In order to use File Shredder:

1. In Explorer, double-click on **Program Files**. Double-click on **File Shredder 98**, then double-click on **File Shredder 98** in the right-hand panel. An information box is displayed, telling you that since this is a shareware version, the program is limited to 100 files. You can choose to register now or later. We recommend that you first use this software before obtaining the license. If it does not suit you, all you have to do is subsequently delete it from your hard disk, without purchasing the license. Click on **Not now** (see Figure 5.6).

Respect the ethics of shareware, purchase the license if you decide to keep the software. If you do not apply this code of conduct, the principle of shareware will not survive!

Figure 5.5 By default, File Shredder is placed in the Program Files folder.

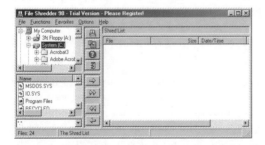

Figure 5.6 File Shredder resembles a traditional file selector.

2. Browse the directories of your hard disk. Click on the file to delete, then click on the right pointing arrow button. The file is selected in the right-hand panel. Repeat these steps for all files to be 'crushed'. When you have finished, press **Delete**. The files are permanently deleted, without a trace. Refer to Help for further information. Close the program when you have finished.

■ Cover your tracks

When you work on your PC, you leave 'tracks', that is, anyone using the same PC can soon find out what you have been working on, which folder has been created, and so on. It is therefore essential to watch out that you do not leave any tracks, and thus protect the confidentiality of your work completely.

Hunting for the informers

On your PC, several items let you quickly view your last work. It is therefore essential to get rid of these nasty telltales regularly.

The first of these items is the Temp folder of Windows, which contains all the latest items in which you have been working, modified items, and so on.

In order to see the contents of the Temp folder, right-click on **Start**. Select **Explore**. Go down in Explorer until the Temp folder is displayed (see Figure 5.7). Click on it. The right-hand panel displays everything contained in this folder. You will see later how to delete it.

The second item is the Documents command, accessible from Start (see Figure 5.8). The last 15 files you have been working on are displayed in the sub-menu of this command. This is a useful function when you want quickly to open a recently-used file, but it is a bit of a shock if you want to protect the confidentiality of your work. You will see later how to delete one or all the files, or even how to delete the Documents command permanently.

The Documents command to your liking

As you have just seen, the Documents command in the Start menu displays the last 15 files used. If you wish to guarantee the confidentiality of your work, it is essential that the

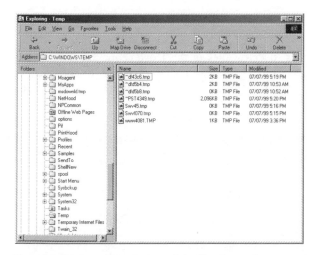

Figure 5.7 The Temp folder displays all the files that you have recently used or modified.

Figure 5.8 The Documents command contains the last 15 files used.

confidential files be deleted from this command. The contents of the command are stored in the Recent folder of Windows.

In order to delete files in the Documents command, right-click on **Start**. Select **Explore**. In Explorer, double-click on **Recent** (see Figure 5.9). The contents of the Documents command are displayed in the right-hand panel. Click on the file to be deleted and press **Delete**.

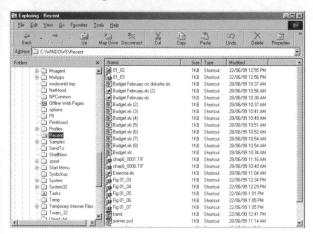

Figure 5.9 Delete quickly a file contained in the Documents command.

 If the Recent folder does not appear in Explorer, click on ***Display***, ***Folder Options***. *Click on the* ***Display*** *tab. In the option* ***Hidden files***, *tick* ***Display all files*** *to activate it. Click on* ***OK*** *to confirm.*

Automatic clean-out of the Documents command

If you want the Documents command to be automatically emptied, without actually deleting it, you can perfectly well display on the Desktop an icon that allows you to empty the Recent folder automatically.

In order to create an icon allowing you to clean out the Recent folder:

1. Click with the right mouse button on the Desktop, then select **New, Text Document** (see Figure 5.10). An icon is displayed on the Desktop and the text is selected. Enter a name for your icon, then press **Enter**.

Figure 5.10 Create a shortcut icon to clean out automatically the Documents command.

2. Click with the right mouse button on the new icon and select **Open**. In the text editor, enter *del c:\windows\recent*.**. Click on **File, Save**. Close Notepad.

From now on, just double-clicking on this icon will automatically empty the contents of the Documents command.

In the batch file editing for cleaning out the Documents command, we are assuming that your operating system is in the Windows folder. If not, adapt the entry to match its name, for example win98, win, and so on.

Deletion of the Documents command

If you wish never to maintain the list of the latest files that you have used, all you have to do is to delete permanently the Recent folder.

In order to delete the Documents command from the Start menu, right-click on **Start**. Select **Explore**. In Explorer, click on **Recent,** then press **Delete**. Confirm the deletion by clicking on **Yes**. From now on, the Document command is deleted.

Deletion of temporary files

You have seen that the Temp folder contains all the files labelled 'temporary'. To protect the confidentiality of your data, it is preferable to delete the contents of this folder.

In order to delete the temporary files, right-click on **Start**. Select **Explore**. In Explorer, double-click on **Temp**. The contents of this folder are displayed in the right-hand panel. Click on the first file of the list, hold down Shift, then click on the last file to be deleted. All the files are selected. Release the key, then press **Delete**.

Automatic deletion of temporary files

If you want the Temp folder to be emptied automatically, you can perfectly well display on the Desktop an icon allowing the Temp folder to be emptied automatically.

In order to create an icon allowing you to empty the Temp folder:

1. Click with the right mouse button on the Desktop, then select **New, Text Document**. An icon is displayed on the Desktop and the text is selected. Enter a name for your icon, then press **Enter**.

2. Click with the right mouse button on the new icon and select **Open**. In the text editor, enter *del c:\windows\temp*.*.* (see Figure 5.11). Click on **File, Save**. Close Notepad.

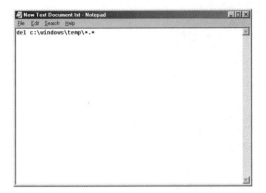

Figure 5.11 Create a shortcut icon to empty the Temp folder automatically.

From now on, all you have to do is double-click on this icon to empty the contents of the Temp folder automatically.

In the editing of the batch file for cleaning out the Documents command, we are presuming that your operating system is contained in the Windows folder. If such is not the case, adapt the entry to match its name, for example win98, win, and so on.

■ Playing hide and seek with items

You will now see how to hide, in Explorer, the files or the folders that you do not wish to be visible.

In order to hide a file in Explorer, right-click on the file concerned and select **Properties**. Click on the **General** tab (see Figure 5.12). Tick the option **Hidden** to activate it. Click on **OK** to confirm.

In order to hide a folder, in Explorer, right-click on the folder concerned and select **Properties**. Click on the **General** tab

Figure 5.12 Hide the files which you wish to remain confidential.

(see Figure 5.13). Tick the **Hidden** option to activate it. Click on **OK** to confirm.

For the files to be really hidden, you have to check that this option is activated.

Figure 5.13 Hide the folders which you wish to remain confidential.

In order to activate the hiding of files, in Explorer, click on **Display, Folder Options.** Click on **View** (see Figure 5.14). Tick the **Do not show hidden files** option to activate it. Click on **OK** to confirm.

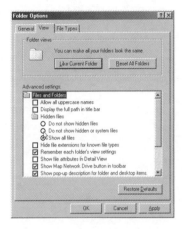

Figure 5.14 Activate the Do not display hidden file options so that they no longer appear in Explorer.

When you wish to display the hidden files again, click on **Display, Folder Options.** Click on **View.** Tick the **Show all files** option to activate it. Click on **OK** to confirm.

6 Anonymity & confidentiality on the Internet

■ ■

Browsing anonymously
Confidentiality of e-mail
Conversing in complete relaxation

In the course of this chapter, you will examine all the possible ways to preserve your anonymity when connected to the Internet and when you are using e-mail.

■ Browsing anonymously

When you share the PC on which you work with other users, it is important that at least some of your explorations on the Web, as well as your e-mail, are not exposed to them. Let us imagine, for example, that you are a conscientious worker, scrupulous and unobtrusive, but you have a small vice: at lunchtime, you love to browse the Web to look at the chassis of the latest model Porsche or of ... Naomi Campbell. You have just finished your browsing and your boss wants to view a particular file. He gets a bit lost though and lands up in History, the record of your browsing .... Well, it's a safe bet that even if you are the most perfect employee in the firm, he won't regard you in the same way any more. Aware that it is essential for you to protect your privacy, above all in your professional context, we have put together a few guidelines that will help you avoid diplomatic incidents of any kind.

Quietly killing the cache

First of all, it is essential that we explain to you the notion of a cache. It has to be admitted, the cache is very nice for the people who wish 'to make savings'. In fact, it lets you store the pages that you have visited in the course of your browsing. The pages visited are split up into files, a file corresponding to an item on the page; for example, one file for the logo, one file for the text, and so on. This possibility is interesting, since it lets you, when you wish to visit this site again, download it more quickly as its items are saved on your hard disk. That's the neat bit, in fact, but there's a downside to everything, and if you wish to preserve your privacy, it is essential to empty this cache.

To understand it better, do as follows if you have Netscape Communicator: go into Explorer, double-click respectively on **Netscape Users, Name of your service provider, Cache,** look at the right-hand panel (see Figure 6.1). All the items of the pages that you have visited are displayed. It is irritating to be betrayed like this, isn't it? Well, let's put this right immediately.

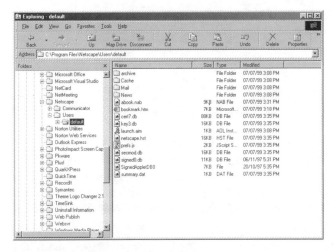

Figure 6.1 View the contents of your cache.

In order to empty the cache of Netscape Communicator:

1. In the browser, click on **Edit, Preferences**. Double-click on **Advanced** in the left-hand panel.

2. Click on **Cache** (see Figure 6.2). Click on **Clear Disk Cache**. Click on **OK** to confirm.

*If you so wish, you can change the folder in which the cached items are saved by clicking on **Choose folder**. You can also change the size of its contents. Remember to click on **OK** to confirm.*

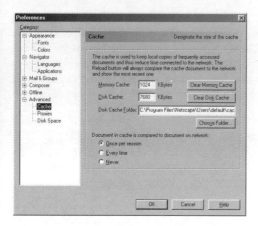

Figure 6.2 Remember to empty your cache.

Emptying the Temporary Internet Files folder

This folder is the equivalent of the cache in Netscape Communicator. In fact, Internet Explorer stores there all the files from the sites that you have visited. It is necessary therefore to empty this folder so as not to give yourself away.

If you have Internet Explorer, take the following steps to view the present contents of your Temporary Internet Files folder, go into Explorer, double-click respectively on **Windows** (or the folder containing your operating system), **Temporary Internet Files,** and look at the right-hand panel (see Figure 6.3). All the items of the pages that you have visited are displayed. Remember to empty this folder regularly.

In order to empty the Temporary Internet Files folder:

1. In the browser, click on **View, Internet Options** (see Figure 6.4).
2. In the Temporary Internet Files panel, click on **Delete files.** Click on **Empty the disk cache.** Click on **OK** in the dialog box which is displayed. Click on **OK** to confirm.

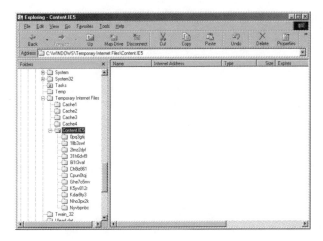

Figure 6.3 View the Temporary Internet Files folder.

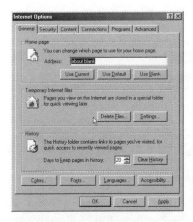

Figure 6.4 Empty the Temporary Internet Files folder so as not to reveal the contents of your browsing.

 Take care not to tick the option to delete the subscriptions when you empty the Temporary Internet Files folder.

Managing the Temporary Internet Files folder

You know already what this folder is for. You can easily personalise its management by deciding, for example, how this folder is filled, the space that it takes up on the hard disk, and so on.

In order to manage the Temporary Internet Files folder:

1. In the browser, click on **View, Internet Options**. In the Temporary Internet Files area, click on **Settings** (see Figure 6.5).

Figure 6.5 View the Temporary Internet Files folder.

2. Define the options desired and choose the size of the disk space used for the contents of the Temporary Internet Files folder (3 % is the most suitable size). Click on **OK** to confirm. Click on **OK** in the Internet Options dialog box.

Gagging the History file

This is another tool which is very nice because it lets you list all the sites that you have visited, and return to them quickly later. Great. Only there is a problem: anyone can find out which sites you have visited and maybe have a quick look at them themselves. We are not censors and we wouldn't dissuade you from visiting such controversial or dangerous sites. On the other hand, we are going to show you how to prevent the History file acting the spoilsport, or even the telltale. The History file exists in both browsers, so we shall show you what to do in both of them.

To appreciate that the History file can be useful as well as harmful, view your own in this way: click on the arrow in the Address bar of your browser, all the sites recently visited are displayed in the form of a list (see Figure 6.6).

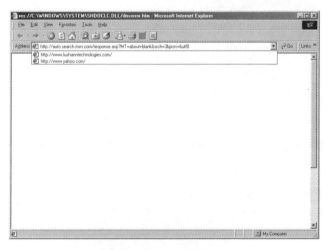

Figure 6.6 View the contents of your History file.

In order to empty the History file in Internet Explorer, click on **View, Internet Options**. Click on **Erase the History file** (see Figure 6.7). Confirm the deletion by clicking on **Yes** in the dialog box which is displayed. Click on **OK** in the Internet Options box.

In order to empty the History file in Netscape Communicator, click on **Edit, Preferences**. Double-click on **Navigator** in the left-hand panel (see Figure 6.8). Click on **Clear history** and click on **Clear location bar**. Confirm the deletion by clicking on **OK** in the dialog box which is displayed. Click on **OK** in the Preferences box.

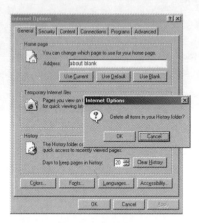

Figure 6.7 Empty the History file in Internet Explorer.

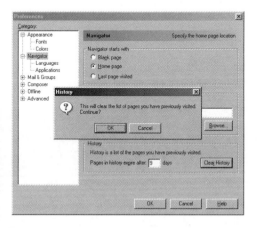

Figure 6.8 Empty the History file in Netscape Communicator.

*You can ask Internet Explorer to empty the History file each time that you close it by clicking on **Tools**, **Internet Options**, then on the **Advanced** tab. Under the **Security** tab, tick the option **Empty Temporary Internet Files folder when browser is closed** to activate it. Click on **OK** to confirm.*

Replying to requests for information

When you surf the Web, it often happens that the site that you are visiting asks your browser for some personal information. The browser informs you by indicating the name of the site and the information requested. You have therefore the possibility of agreeing or not to give this information. However, the higher the level of protection, the more 'sensitive' these requests will be. We therefore are showing you how to opt for an optimal level of security.

In order to activate maximum security in Internet Explorer, click on **View, Internet Options**. Click on the **Security** tab. In the Zone panel, click on the arrow and select **Internet** (see Figure 6.9) and then select the **High** option. Click on **OK** to confirm.

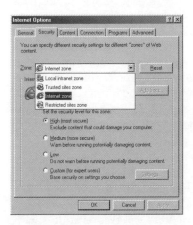

Figure 6.9 Opt for maximum security when you surf the Internet.

From now on, whatever the nature of the information requested, you will be automatically informed by a dialog box. Reply to the requests in the knowledge that:

- **Authorize** lets you agree to the transmission of all of the data.

- **Authorize** also allows you, by disabling certain options, to send only the data that you have selected.

- **Refuse** lets you prohibit the transmission of data.

■ Confidentiality of e-mail

If it is correct that e-mail is a considerable step forward in the concept of the communication, it also has certain drawbacks which it is impossible to ignore, beginning with the e-mail address which reveals a great deal. In fact, it always has the same format: the name (usually your own), the name of your access provider (revealing or what?); and finally the place where you are located in the domain name – as far as confidentiality is concerned, it's a dead loss! Moreover, the Trash or Items deleted folder, which we all have an annoying tendency to forget about, takes its revenge regularly for our lack of attention to it: it lets anyone view precisely the messages that we have discarded! In short, we have not won yet. Here are therefore a few steps to take to protect you and preserve your privacy, even your anonymity.

Permanent deletion of messages

You know that whatever your e-mail software, you have a folder which is the equivalent of the Recycle Bin in Windows. Thus, as soon as you throw away a message by clicking on it then pressing Delete, it is automatically stored in this folder. This is very useful for the absent minded who throw away a wrong item, since in this way they can recover it. It is more of an annoyance for those who are self-confident and decisive in deleting unwanted messages, since they are in danger of forgetting to empty the Recycle Bin before exiting the e-mail program.

The folder storing the deleted items is called Trash in Messenger and Items deleted in Outlook Express. In Outlook Express, you can choose to empty automatically this folder each time that you exit the e-mail program. This is not available in Messenger – which is a real nuisance – so take care to empty the Trash folder each time you exit this program.

In order to empty automatically the **Deleted Items folder** in Outlook Express, click on **Tools, Options** (see Figure 6.10). Tick the **Empty messages from the 'Deleted Items' folder on exit** option to activate it, then click on **OK** to confirm.

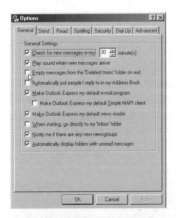

Figure 6.10 Empty the Deleted Items folder automatically in Outlook Express.

Sending messages anonymously

It is obvious that it is virtually impossible to preserve one's anonymity when using one's own e-mail address. In fact, as we explained earlier in this chapter, the address is very revealing, since most of the time it is composed of your name, sometimes your company's name, the name of your service provider and the country where you are located. It is the equivalent of a postal address. The good news is that, just as for letters addressed to a P.O. box, which represents a guarantee of confidentiality, there is a similar kind of service available for electronic mail. Perhaps you are one of those who are wondering why it should be necessary to protect one's anonymity on the Web. This debate is as vast as the Internet itself: if one considers the free circulation of ideas to be essential, why claim anonymity? On the other hand, why should one not be able to have the right to be protected from neurotics and other nosy parkers? Each of you will respond to this according to your own use of the Internet. It is not for us to lecture you on the need for anonymity on the Internet; we simply consider that this point is important in the context of sharing and protection, which is what this book is about.

The first of the solutions to retain one's anonymity on the Internet is to use a re-mailer. You send the message to the re-mailer, who passes it on, equipping your message with an anonymous sender, before sending it on to the addressee. In order to obtain the list of the re-mailers, launch a search on the Web by entering *re-mailer* in the search box and contact the one that suits you.

You can also use a program allowing you to send e-mail anonymously, post articles to news groups without revealing your address and surf incognito on the Web. One of these programs is Private idaho, which, as well as being very useful, has the advantage of being completely free. You can obtain it at the following address: **www.eskimo.com./~joelm/pi.html**. We cannot describe exactly the procedures for using Private idaho in this book, for lack of space, but we offer you a summary of the main points in configuring this program. Consult the program's Help function for further information.

In order to configure Private idaho, after installing it, click on **File, Options**. Enter your e-mail address, then your name. In the SMTP server name box, enter the name of the outgoing mail server and in the POP3 server name box, enter the name of the incoming mail server. To finish, enter the user name under which the program opens a session for collecting e-mail. Click on **OK** to confirm.

In order to use Private idaho, after composing your message according to the normal way (addressee, subject, and so on), select the name of the re-mailer desired in the list Remailer name. Click on **OK** to confirm. Private idaho prepares to send your message. Click on **Send** to send the message.

■ Conversing in complete relaxation

If you are one of the lucky devils taking part in Internet Chat or in Newsgroups, you already know that these new methods of communication have great advantages, considering their costs as much as their universality. However, they also present certain inconveniences: it is easier to let yourself go when you are hidden! That's why you can consider that the Internet discussion forums are like a particularly smutty version of *All you ever wanted to know about sex without ever daring to ask*. This isn't necessarily disagreeable as long as you are consenting. It is exasperating, though, if what you wanted was to initiate a discussion on the latest performance of the *Marriage of Figaro* at Covent Garden! And it is not just sex that gets the little dears all worked up; the mixed up, the sad and the obsessive of all kinds have a great time here! You will find in the following pages some tips and tricks to prevent you from getting too bored, annoyed or even pestered.

Respecting the rules

If you wish to participate in discussion groups or in real time discussions using Chat, respect certain rules of conduct, which will help you avoid upsetting certain people.

Rules to respect in conversations on the Internet:

- Never write in capital letters; the participants interpret this as shouting.

- Remember to greet the participants when you arrive, it makes a good impression.

- Don't send any white (empty) lines to attract attention, it disturbs the course of the conversation and annoys everyone.

- Keep to the subject, if there is one. In live chat, avoid talking about the impressionists if you are taking part in a group to do with cubism and the art of Picasso.

- Don't automatically discuss in an aside, the other participants would take it amiss (remember that you yourself don't appreciate 'muttering').

- Avoid sentences which are too long, this is electronic communication, not Charles Dickens. The more brief and concise you are, the better!

- If you do not want to be e-mailed by one of the participants, don't reveal your real address, or else provide a secondary address when you enter the conversation.

Disregard the troublemakers

When you are chatting, it happens sometimes that one of the participants uses you as a scapegoat. If the method of loftily ignoring it doesn't work, you have to act. Here is how to do it using the mIRC program. This is a shareware program that you can obtain on the Web at the address **www.mirc.co.uk**. It is the most used on the Internet, since it is simple to use and offers a graphical interface like Windows.

To ignore a troublemaker with mIRC, click on **Commands, Ignore user profile** (see Figure 6.11). Enter the name of the participant to ignore in the option Enter nick-name. Click on **OK** to confirm.

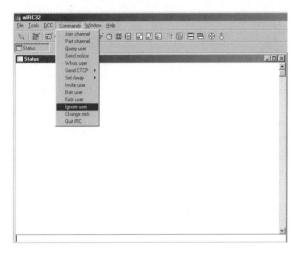

Figure 6.11 Disregard the morons with mIRC.

Part

III

Protecting the PC against crashes, mishandling and external attack

■ ■

When you have a computer that contains all your personal and professional data, you obviously treat it as the apple of your eye.

The next five chapters are going to deal with protecting your PC, its system as well as its data, and your browsing on the Internet. We are offering you therefore, 'in this world full of danger', a few ways to ensure the maximum security of all your essential data.

7
Protecting your system

Principles of starting Windows
Protecting the access to your system
Protecting key points of your system
System maintenance

The notion of protection begins as soon as you switch on your computer. In fact, as soon as your operating system starts, the first weak points can be accessed by any hacker who wants to penetrate your system, or else by any virus determined to sow panic in your PC. It is therefore essential to protect these extremely sensitive stages. In the course of this chapter, you will find out absolutely everything about protecting your system.

■ Principles of starting Windows

To comprehend fully the contents of the different sections, it is vital that you understand the process of starting up your system.

First of all, it is the BIOS (*Basic Input Output System*) which makes all the running, by indicating to the machine the different settings for starting up. Next, it is the operating system Io.sys that takes over the baton. It works in DOS, but nevertheless is an integral part of Windows. The Io can also be called Winboot. In this case, a DOS program with its own start files is already active and Windows 98 has included Io.sys in the Winboot.sys. In reality, it is a game of permanent hide and seek; they hide from one another. Next, Io.sys starts the drivers it needs, such as Himem, Server, Ifship, and so on. This automatic process lets you record the right entries in the system file Config.sys. From this moment, it is the **Msdos.sys** file that begins its work, by determining the start mode of Windows 98. Next, it is the turn of the drivers and settings to take their places. Windows is finally launched and its graphical interface is loaded. At this stage, you are asked, more often than not, to enter a password. A final formality, the contents of the Install folder are processed. Did you know that so many things happened between the moment when you press the button to switch on your computer and the Windows desktop appearing?

Protecting yourself from start-up problems by planning ahead

When you switch on your computer and launch Windows, the boot sequence is first going to look for the start code, then check whether there is a floppy disk in A drive. If there is, then the BIOS looks for a boot sector on the floppy, and, if it finds one, it starts the system from the floppy. If it fails to find a floppy, it then tries to start from the active partition of the hard disk. When the hard disk has a problem and Windows refuses to load, the only solution is to insert a startup disk (boot disk) which will let you start your system. When Windows was being installed, the Wizard asked if you wanted to create a startup disk; if you said yes, you are already the happy owner of the miracle disk; you just have to insert it into the floppy drive and Windows will load. If you did not create this disk, there is still time to do so before catastrophe strikes.

In order to create a startup disk:

1. Insert a formatted disk in your disk drive. Insert the CD-ROM of Windows 98 in your CD-ROM drive.

2. Click on **Start, Settings, Control Panel**. Double-click on **Add/Remove Programs**. Click on the **Startup Disk** tab (see Figure 7.1 on page 112).

3. Click on **Create Disk**. Click **OK**. Close the Control Panel.

You are now equipped to face any startup problems; inserting this disk when you switch on the computer is the only effective solution.

■ Protecting the access to your system

You have just seen how the start of Windows works. You are now going to study a few procedures for protecting the access to your system by putting a block in the way, so that no one can penetrate your PC without your authorisation.

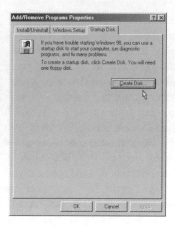

Figure 7.1 Create a Windows startup disk.

Protecting the BIOS by a password

Remember to note the name of the manufacturer of your BIOS, since this may be useful in case of a catastrophe.

The first procedure is to block access to the BIOS with a password. If you have carefully read the section 'Principles of starting Windows', you know how important the loading of the BIOS is: without it, no system, just a boring blank screen.

In order to set up a password for the BIOS, switch on your computer, then hold down the **Delete** key all the while the RAM is loading. The DOS window of Figure 7.2 is displayed. Select **Password Settings** using the cursor keys (the mouse doesn't work, obviously). Press **Enter**. Enter a password (see Figure 7.3). Press the **Escape** key. Press the **N (no)** key in the box asking if you wish to exit without saving changes, then press **Enter**.

From now on, you have to enter this password to authorise the start of Windows.

STANDARD CMOS	INTEGRATED PERIPHERALS
BIOS FEATURES SETUP	PASSWORD SETTINGS
CHIPSET FEATURES SETUP	IDE HDD AUTO DETECTION
PNP/PCI CONFIGURATION	SAVE & EXIT SETUP
LOAD SETUP DEFAULTS	EXIT WITHOUT SAVING

Figure 7.2 Display the BIOS setup.

Figure 7.3 Create a password for the BIOS.

Disaster, you have forgotten the password for your BIOS

As far as disasters go, you can't get much worse: you can't get into your computer at all if you have forgotten the password of your BIOS. We won't hide from you that the following procedure is a bit hard. If you are no good with a screwdriver, leave it and contact the person who sold you the machine. Get him to read the following, and he will do the procedure himself.

- **Instructions for 'trouble-shooters'.** Open the machine and locate the battery on the motherboard. Remove it from its slot. Leave it like that for a few days (three or four) so that the EPROM containing the password empties itself, since it has no more power. Reinstall the battery in its slot and switch on the computer. Since the password has now been forgotten, you no longer have a problem. On the other hand, you have to reconfigure all your peripherals!

- **Instructions for 'old machines'.** Locate the switch on the motherboard corresponding to the password (refer to the technical manual that you have religiously kept). Open the machine, disable the switch. The password is disabled.

- **Instructions for the Internet.** Visit the site of the manufacturer of your BIOS (see tip in 'Protecting the BIOS by a password') and get hold of the manufacturer password, since it overrides your own password. All you have to do is enter this password instead of your own. The BIOS is unblocked!

Don't change the Boot sequence

You saw, at the start of this chapter, that the instant you turn on your computer, the Boot sequence engages; which is as if your computer is warming up. By default, this takes place in the order A: then C:, which means that the computer begins by trying to boot from a floppy disk. You will see in many books that it is advisable to change the Boot sequence so that it begins with Drive C:, so as to speed up the loading of Windows. Do not make this change! Imagine that you had startup problems, the disk would be no help at all, since the Boot sequence would begin with Drive C: and would find ...nothing!

Frightening off intruders

You have decided not to set up a BIOS password; you are probably right. This is a bit risky, if you are an absent-minded sort. There are other solutions to prevent undesirables from penetrating your system. Of course, this type of block isn't for everyday use, since it would be too fiddly to use; only employ this procedure when you have to be away for a certain length of time.

You are going create a file which is going to block the system and which will be able to, with a bit of humour, frighten undesirables who will try to switch on your computer, whilst you are enjoying the sun in the Caribbean or the green of the Yorkshire Dales.

In order to block Windows:

1. Click on **Start, Run** (see Figure 7.4). Enter *Notepad* and press **Enter**.
2. Enter some lines of text, such as:

   @ECHO You are not welcome!

Figure 7.4 Create a file blocking the start of Windows.

@ECHO In a few seconds, this computer will self-destruct.

loop

@goto

3. Click on **File, Save As**. Select the root directory of your hard disk (C:) and name the file *win.bat*. Click on **Save**. Close Notepad.

From now on, the computer will freeze on C: and display the message that you have entered (see Figure 7.5).

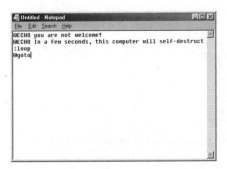

Figure 7.5 Rather frightening for the comedians who want to use your hard disk.

In order to access your computer on your return, switch it on and press **F8** as the ROM loads to open the Start menu. Select the option **Command line only** (with the cursor keys).

If need be, enter *CD.* and press **Enter** to changer directory
and return to the root directory of the disk. At the DOS
prompt, enter *del win.bat* so that the blocking file is deleted.
Press **Enter**. Windows loads.

■ Protecting key points of your system

Now that you know how to block access to Windows, you
have to see how to block access to other vital items of the
system and how to protect them. Although the procedures
indicated above are reliable, the fact is that they are a bit
complicated and a bit restricting. After all, you can tolerate
others using your system under certain safeguards. Here are
a few of them.

Hide the Start menu

The Start menu is displayed by pressing **F8**, just as the RAM
loads. This menu lets you have access to a certain number of
options, vital for your system (see Figure 7.6). The way to
prevent accidents is to hide this menu and thus prevent access
to it.

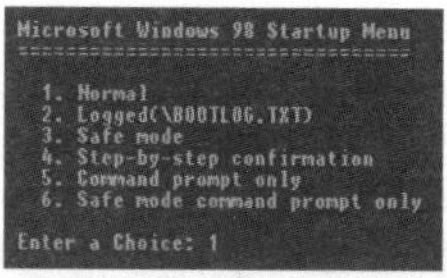

Figure 7.6 The Start menu offers a number of absolutely vital options.

In order to hide the Start menu:

1. You first have to display the system files. In order to do
   this, click on **Display, Folder Options** in Explorer or My
   Computer. Click on the **Display** tab. Tick the **Display all
   the files** option to activate it (see Figure 7.7). Click on **OK**
   to confirm.

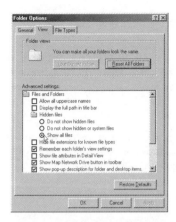

Figure 7.7 Display your system files in Explorer.

2. Click on **Start, Run**. Enter *Notepad* and press Enter. Click on **File, Open**. In the dialog box, click on the arrow of the **Type** option and select **All**. Activate the root directory of the hard disk (C:). Right click on the **Msdos.sys** file (see Figure 7.8) and select **Properties**. Disable the **Read only** option. Click on **OK** to confirm, then click on **Open**.

Figure 7.8 Authorise the changes in the Msdos.sys file.

■■■

3. In the [Options] area, enter *BootKeys=0*. Click on **File**, **Save**. Close Notepad.

Access to the Start menu is blocked. In order to reinstate it, repeat the procedure as above, then delete the *BootKeys=0* line.

Hide the system files

The system files are vital for the functioning of Windows: without them, nothing works, Windows gets all mixed up! It is therefore preferable to hide these files so that no one can destroy them. That being so, remember to save them on a disk just in case the 'attackers' know the trick for displaying them again.

First of all, and so that you can save them, be aware of the files which are vital for the good functioning of your Windows. Here is the list of them (see Figure 7.9):

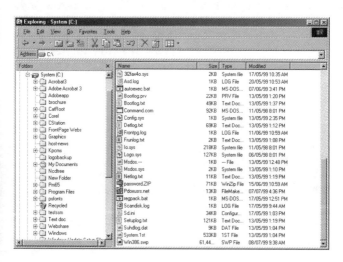

Figure 7.9 The system files are stored in the root directory of your hard disk and in the Windows folder.

- Config.sys;
- Msdos.sys;
- Autoexec.bat;
- Io.sys;
- Winboot.sys;
- Progman.ini;
- Win.ini;
- Protocol.ini;
- System.ini.

In order to hide the system files, click on **Display, Folder Options** in Explorer or My Computer. Click on the **Display tab**. Tick the **Do not display system files or hidden files** option. Click on **OK** to confirm.

Back up your sensitive files

Above all, remember to make backups on disk or other media of your important files. If a disaster happens (hard disk crash, inadvertent formatting, and so on), you still have a way out. You must therefore absolutely remember to back up your most sensitive files, even if it seems a big hassle.

Print a report system

The main difficulty, when you have to reinstall an operating system, lies in the fact that you will not remember all the configuration techniques of all your extension cards. It will be impossible for you to remember the IRQ of the sound card, the card's memory address, and so on. To save time, it is preferable to print all the basic data of your system. Thus, you will have the benefit of optimal security.

In order to print a system report, right-click on **My Computer** and select **Properties**. Click on the **Device Manager** tab (see Figure 7.10). Click on **Print**. Tick the **All devices and system summaries** option. Click on **OK** to begin printing.

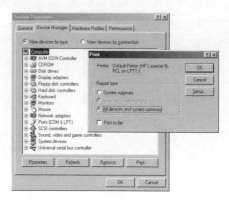

Figure 7.10 Print a report of your system.

Check the system files

Windows 98 offers a utility that checks the state of your system files. Using it regularly, you will be prepared against any possible problems, ensuring the protection of your system.

In order to check your system files, click on **Start, Programs, Accessories, System Tools, System Information** (see Figure 7.11). Click on **Tools, System File Checker** (see Figure 7.12). If need be, tick the option **Scan for altered files**, then click on **Settings** (see Figure 7.13). Define your choice in the different tabs. Click on **OK** to confirm. Click on **Start** to run the check.

Figure 7.11 The Information system window shows your hard disk settings.

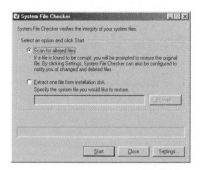

Figure 7.12 Define the type of check to activate for the system files.

Figure 7.13 Set the options for checking your system files.

■ System maintenance

To keep your car in perfect working order, you make sure it is maintained, don't you? In the same way, if you want to protect your system as best you can and you wish for it to last for a long time and work correctly, you have to maintain your computer. In the following section, you will learn about certain procedures to ensure perfect maintenance of your system.

ScanDisk

ScanDisk lets you correct physical and logical errors on your hard disk. Next, it can repair the damaged areas if you wish.

In order to launch ScanDisk, click on **Start**, **Programs**, **Accessories**, **System Tools**, **ScanDisk** (see Figure 7.14). Choose the type of analysis desired, then click on **Start**. Click on **OK** to launch the scan of your disk.

Figure 7.14 Launch ScanDisk to detect possible physical errors on your hard disk.

Defragmentation

Do you know how saving your files works at the level of the disk? Of you don't, here is the explanation for a better understanding of the principle of defragmentation and its usefulness. The hard disk is divided into sectors; this function is called partition. When you save files, they are stored on your hard disk in dispersed and discontinuous pieces; which means that your hard disk is fragmented. This fragmentation has the inconvenience of slowing down the disk, since it has to make numerous stops to find the different pieces of a file. **Before** protecting your hard disk, it is preferable **from time to time** to **defragment** it.

For this, click on **Start, Programs, Accessories, System Tools, Disk defragmenter**. Define the disk to **defragment** in the **box at the top**. Click on Settings (see Figure 7.15). Define the **defragmentation** option desired, then click on **OK** to confirm. Wait until the defragmentation is finished. Click on **Quit** when it is finished.

Figure 7.15 Defragment your hard disk for it to work in optimal conditions.

Maintenance Wizard

Now that you have studied the different procedures to follow to protect your hard disk from crashes and others problems, we are going to present in this section a utility allowing you to schedule the different maintenance tasks. Thus, **once** you have defined the task and scheduled it, you do not have to bother with any of it, since Windows takes care of everything!

In order to define automatic maintenance:

1. Double-click on **My Computer**, then on **Scheduled tasks**. In the window that is displayed, double-click on **Creating a scheduled task**. Click on **Next** in the first stage. The second stage lets you select the **task** to be carried out (see Figure 7.16). Click on the maintenance task desired, then click on **Next**.

2. In the new stage, select the **frequency** desired (**every day, every week,** and so on) and click on **Next**. Define **the time** for beginning the **task**, the days and the starting date for carrying out this **task**. Click on **Next**. Click on **Finish**.

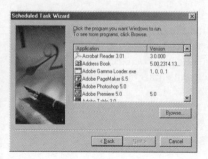

Figure 7.16 Select the maintenance task to be carried out.

From now on, the **maintenance tasks** of your disk will begin automatically on the dates and at the times programmed.

*In order to change a scheduled maintenance **task**, double-click on **My Computer**, then on **Scheduled tasks**. Double-click on the **task** to change, then edit the settings in the dialog box which is displayed. Click on **OK** to confirm.*

8 Protecting your data

Backing up your data

Restoring your data

Write-protecting and/or hiding items

In the course of this chapter, you are going to discover all the procedures that allow you to protect your data in the best way. In fact, it is advisable to protect all the vital system data as well as all the files, folders, and so on, which are precious to you.

■ Backing up your data

After a certain time of use, your PC will store all the data of your professional and personal activities. So, to avoid any disaster in case of a problem with the hard disk, remember to do regular backups of your data.

Data compression

The first procedure is to save your data independently. For example, every year you have to do your accounts, which are filed in a folder. You are not immune to accidental damage, so it is preferable to make a backup on disk. That being so, when a folder is very large, it will not fit on a single disk. The solution is to compress the data with a utility that reduces the space used by the folder. The most well known shareware program for compressing data is WinZip. Launch a search on the Web to find sites where you can download this program. Download it on to your hard disk and proceed with the installation.

In order to compress data with WinZip:

1. In Explorer, right-click on the folder or file concerned (see Figure 8.1). Select **Add to Zip**. Click on **I agree** in the dialog box which is displayed.

   The dialog box of Figure 8.2 is displayed.

Figure 8.1 Select the command Add to Zip in the shortcut menu of the folder or file.

Figure 8.2 Tell WinZip what it is that you wish to compress.

*You can add a password to your compression procedures. Thus, no one but you will be able to decompress the folder. To set this up, click on **Password** in the **Add** dialog box. Enter the password desired and click on **OK**. Follow the traditional methods for compressing a folder.*

2. In the Add dialog, the option **Add to archive** displays the name of the folder or file selected followed by the extension **.zip**. Click on **Add**. If you wish to change the name of the folder of compression, click on **New**, enter the new name and click on **OK**.

The contents of the folder or file are zipped. The progression of the compression is displayed in the status bar. Once the compression is finished, the WinZip window displays the list of files contained in the compressed folder (see Figure 8.3).

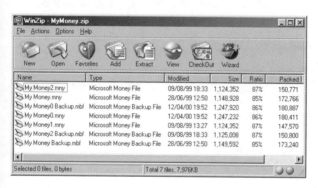

Figure 8.3 The WinZip window displays the list of files contained in the compressed folder.

3. Close WinZip.

Now the folder has been compressed, you can save it to disk.

*To decompress a folder or a file, right-click on the folder or file concerned, and select **Extract to**. Click on **I agree** in the dialog box which is displayed. Then click on **Extract** in the next dialog box. Close WinZip.*

Copying data with Backup

Windows offers, among its system tools, a utility for backing up data, called Backup. It has to be admitted that Backup is definitely a rather fiddly and long-winded program to use, but it is essential if you wish to protect your data to the maximum and avoid losing everything in case of a hard disk crash.

Before studying the procedures for using Backup, here are a few points about the Backup tool:

- Do not try to restore a complete backup of your system. In fact, you would run the risk of overwriting your Registry.

- The Backup tool of Windows 98 does not recognise the backups in QIC format, which was the previous standard for backups created in MS-DOS or in version 3.x of Windows.

- Close the window of Backup.exe when making the backup of your data: you will reduce the waiting time slightly.

In order to backup your data:

1. Click on **Start, Programs, Accessories, System Tools, Backup**. In the dialog box displayed, tick the option **Create a new backup job** to activate it and click on **OK**.

2. In the second stage, tick the option **Tools Backup Wizard** to activate it and click on **Next**. Tick now the option desired for the backup, being aware that:

   - **Back up my Computer** lets you arrange the backup of all the files on your local drive(s).

   - **Back up selected files** lets you choose the files or folders that you wish to back up.

3. Click on **Next**. If you have chosen to select the files, you have to do it now. Click on **OK** when you have finished. Next, the Wizard asks you to indicate the location for backing up your files. Click on **Next**.

4. In the new stage, tick the option desired, then click on **Next**. Name your backup and click on **Start**.

5. The backup begins and its progress is displayed. When the backup is finished, click on **OK**.

Forget Microsoft Backup

It has to be admitted, and without any prejudice on our part, Microsoft Backup isn't a very user-friendly tool. Not that it is unreliable, but it is very long-winded and the procedure is fiddly. You might therefore choose to get hold of more powerful backup software, such as Iomega.zip. Once you have installed this new backup program, you will be confronted by a small problem: if you try to launch it by invoking the Properties command, then by clicking on the Tools tab, you will only have the MS Backup program available. Here is how to proceed to access the new backup program.

To use a different backup program, right-click on **Start**, select **Open** (see Figure 8.4). Double-click on **Programs**, then open the folder in which the backup program is located. Click with the right mouse button on the backup program and select **Properties**. Click on the **Shortcut** tab, then, in the Target box, right-click and choose **Select all**. Repeat this procedure, but this time select **Copy**.

Figure 8.4 Display the contents of the Start menu.

Now, you have to edit the Backup button, which by default launches the program Microsoft Backup. To do this, click on **Start, Run**. Enter *regedit* and press **Enter**. In the Registry, click on **Edit, Find** (see Figure 8.5). Type *mycomputer* in the box and press **Enter** to confirm. Double-click on **My Computer**. If you do not see the command **backuppath**, click on **Edit, New, Key**. Name it *backuppath* and press **Enter**. In the right-hand panel, double-click on **backuppath**. In the Data field of the value, press **Ctrl+V** to paste what you placed on the Clipboard. Press **Enter**. You have modified the preceding procedure with the path for the new backup program.

Figure 8.5 Change the name of the backup program in the Registry.

From now on, to call up the new backup program, all you have to do is click on **Backup now**.

■ Restoring your data

It is quite obvious that, if you encounter problems with your hard disk, you will have to restore the data from the backup. The procedure is relatively simple, since it can be done with the help of a Wizard. The steps below show the restoration of data backed up with Microsoft Backup.

In order to restore data:

1. Launch Microsoft Backup. In the Microsoft Backup window, select **Tools, Restoration Wizard**. In the first stage, select the source files of the backup from the **Restore from list**, then click on **Next**.

2. A Wizard displays the list of backup files found on the medium that you indicated. Tick the box of each backup operation that you wish to restore and click **OK**.

The Wizard creates a list of the drives, folders and files contained in the backup operations chosen.

3. Tick the items to be restored and click on **Next**. Then tell the Wizard the location where you wish to place the restored files. (**Original location** or **Other location**). Click on **Next** after having, possibly, specified the new location. Click on **Start** to begin restoration.

Recovering binned items

When you have binned one or more items by mistake, you have the possibility of recovering them from the Recycle Bin. For this, all you have to do is to click on the file to be restored, then click on **File, Restore**. However, you may have emptied the Recycle Bin and ... it may no longer be possible to recover the binned files. Windows has thought of everything, you still have the possibility of using Undelete, which is going to sweep the hard disk in order to recover the items binned. There are other utilities for this type of recovery, such as Norton Utilities. Possibly get what you are after by browsing on the Web.

In order to restore items binned by mistake, insert the Windows CD-ROM into your CD-ROM drive. Look for the file Undelete.exe and copy it into the Command folder of Windows. Restart the computer in MS-DOS mode by clicking on **Start, Shut down, Restart in MS-DOS mode** (see Figure 8.6). At the DOS prompt, enter *cd nameoffoldercontainingthedeletedfiles* and press **Enter**. Enter *undelete* and press **Enter**. The system displays all the files that it has been able to recover. In order to restore a file, press on the **O** key and indicate the first letter of its name. Exit from MS-DOS mode: your files are restored to their original location.

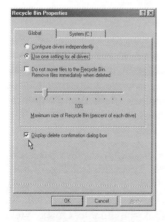

Figure 8.6 Restore your files with Undelete.exe.

Confirmation of deletion

You have seen in the course of previous chapters that the Recycle Bin can contain the files that you have deleted. To be on the safe side, it is also preferable to activate a dialog box asking you to confirm the deletion; in this way, it will be highly unlikely that you will bin items by mistake.

In order to activate the request for confirmation of deletion:

1. Click with the right mouse button on the Recycle Bin. Select **Properties** (see Figure 8.7).

Figure 8.7 Ask Windows to display a dialog box to confirm the deletion.

2. Tick the **Display delete confirmation dialog box** option. Click on **OK** to confirm.

From now on, when you delete an item, the dialog box of Figure 8.8 will be displayed. You will have to confirm or cancel the deletion.

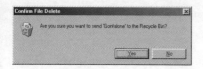

Figure 8.8 Confirm the deletion by clicking on Yes.

■ Write-protecting and/or hiding items

In order to prevent anyone from messing with your data without your permission, you can write-protect certain items. Thus, only the people authorised will be able to access your data.

Preventing the quick view

You know that when you right-click on any file, a command is offered in the shortcut menu, called Quick View. This command lets you open the file in Quick View and thus see the contents without actually opening the file within its application. If you want no one to see the contents of your files, it is preferable to disable this command.

In order to disable Quick View, in Explorer, click on **View, Folder Options**. Click on the **File Types** tab (see Figure 8.9). In the list **Registered File types,** click on the type of document to which you wish to prevent Quick View access. Click on **Edit** (see Figure 8.10). Click on the **Enable Quick View** option to disable it. Click on **OK** to confirm. Click on **OK** in the **Folder Options** box.

Figure 8.9 The File Types tab lets you change the commands offered in the shortcut menu of files, folders, and so on.

Figure 8.10 Disable Quick View for the type of document desired.

Hiding and/or write-protecting files

You can tell Windows that some of your essential files must be neither visible nor modifiable. Here is the procedure to apply.

In order to hide a file, in Explorer, right-click on the file and select **Properties**. In the **General** tab, click on the option **Hidden** (see Figure 8.11). Click on **OK** to confirm.

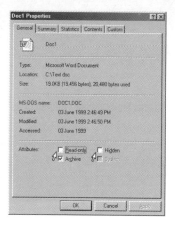

Figure 8.11 Hide the files that you wish to keep secret.

 *The **Hidden** option will only be active if you have told Explorer not to display hidden files. To this effect, click on **View**, **Folder Options**. Click on the **View** tab. Tick the option **Do not show system or hidden files**. Click on **OK** to confirm.*

You can, of course, leave a file visible, but prohibit anyone from interfering with its contents.

In order to write-protect a file, in Explorer, right-click on the file and select **Properties**. In the **General** tab, click on the **Read-only** option. Click on **OK** to confirm.

Hiding and/or write-protecting folders

Just as for files, you can ask Windows to make some of your essential folders neither visible nor modifiable. Here is what to do.

In order to hide a folder, in Explorer, right-click on the folder concerned and select **Properties**. In the **General** tab, go to **Attributes**, click on the **Hidden** option (see Figure 8.12). Click on **OK** to confirm.

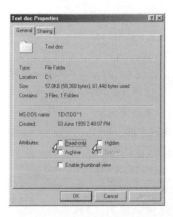

Figure 8.12 Hide the folders that you wish to keep secret.

You can, of course, leave a folder visible, but forbid any one to tamper with its contents.

In order to write-protect a folder, in Explorer, right-click on the folder concerned and select **Properties**. In the **General** tab, click on the **Read-only** option. Click on **OK** to confirm.

Write-protecting the Control Panel

As you know, the Control Panel contains a whole heap of icons that let you configure the environment. If you do not want anybody to have access to the various icons of your

Control Panel, you have to hide it. Thus, you keep your personal settings for these the icons and no one else will be able to change them.

In order to hide Control Panel icons:

1. Click on **Start, Run**. Type in *control.ini* and press Enter (see Figure 8.13). Locate the section [don't load] then enter the commands letting you hide the icons followed by =*no* , bearing in mind that:

   ■ **Display** is called DESK.CPL.

   ■ **Add New Hardware** is called SYSDM.CPL.

   ■ **Add/Remove programs** is called APPWIZ.CPL.

   ■ **Date/Time** is called TIMEDATE.CPL.

   ■ **Internet Options** is called INAND SO ONPL.CPL.

   ■ **Game Controllers** is called JOY.CPL.

   ■ **Modems** is called MODEM.CPL.

   ■ **Passwords** is called PASSWORD.CPL.

   ■ **Multimedia** and **Sounds** are called MMSYS.CPL.

   ■ **Regional Settings** is called INTL.CPL.

   ■ **Network** is called NAND SO ONPL.CPL.

   ■ **Mouse, Keyboard, Printers, Power Management** are called MAIN.CPL.

   ■ **Themes** is called THEMES.CPL.

2. Finally, save the file and close Notepad.

From now on, the modules listed in the file Control.ini will no longer be displayed in the Control Panel. In order to reactivate them, open the file Control.ini and delete the blocking line (for example THEMES.CPL=no).

Figure 8.13 It is the file Control.ini that lets you hide Control Panel modules.

Hiding properties, tabs, and so on

To prevent anyone from interfering in your absence with the properties of My Computer or your folders and files, you can choose to block access to the Properties dialog box or to certain tabs.

When you change items in the Registry, remember to back up the section on which you are going to operate. Thus, if you encounter the slightest problem, you will be able quickly to restore the original version with the help of the backup.

In order to hide the properties, tabs, and so on:

1. Click on **Start, Run**. Enter *regedit* and press Enter. Double-click on **HKEY_CURRENT_USER** then on **Software, Microsoft, Windows, Current Version, Policies** (see Figure 8.14).

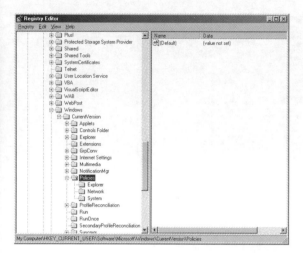

Figure 8.14 Hide the properties, tabs, and so on, of your items.

2. In the right-hand panel, double-click on **System**. Hide the items according to your requirements, bearing in mind that:

- **NoDispCPL** disables the display properties.

- **NoDispSerSavPage** hides the Screen saver tab.

- **NoDispSettingsPage** hides the Configuration tab.

- **NoDispBackgroundPage** hides the Background tab.

- **NoVirtMemPage** hides Virtual memory in the Performance tab.

- **NoAdminPage** hides the RemoteAdministration tab in the Password module.

- **NoConfigPage** hides the tab Hardware Profiles in the System module.

- **NoDispAppearancePage** hides the Appearance tab.

3. After disabling the different options by entering *=0* for each of them, save, then close the Registry editor.

In order to reactivate the properties, tabs, and so on, repeat the procedures indicated above and reactivate the options by replacing =0 with *=1*. Save, then close the Registry.

9 Protecting yourself from the Internet

■ ■

Protecting your browsing

Protecting payment on the Internet

Protecting e-mail

Although it is true that the Internet is a brilliant communication tool, it is nevertheless essential to configure certain security options to reduce the risks to the minimum, since it is undeniably risky to download software, or visit sites containing ActiveX and other Java applications. In the course of this chapter, you will see all the measures to take so as not to run any risks when you are using the Net.

■ Protecting your browsing

Be aware that the Internet is an area of almost total freedom where you find the worst along with the best. The designers of the two main browsers, namely Netscape and Microsoft, have made it a point of honour to offer as many options as possible and imaginable to make your use of the Internet as safe as it can be. In fact, it would be dangerous, even irresponsible, to browse without having arranged maximum protection. You will find in the following section all the tips and tricks to learn to armour-plate your browser.

Security Certificates

The certificate is the security feature offered by Navigator, the browser module of Netscape Communicator. Although it is true that it is less flexible in use than the security zones offered by Internet Explorer, the fact remains that it is this concept which is surely the most reliable solution in the long run. The principle of the certificate consists of allocating one to each communication partner, through an independent authority. Hence, the certificate guarantees the identity of the person and fixes the access rights of each partner. When you browse, the browser checks whether the Website possesses a certificate, and regulates the access in consequence.

In order to see the security information in Navigator, click on **Communicator, Security Information**. In the left-hand panel, click on the security item for which you require information (see Figure 9.1).

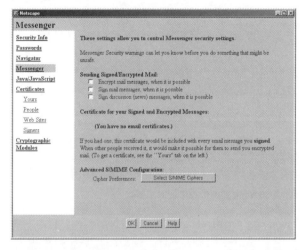

Figure 9.1 Open the Security Information window to find the information that is of interest to you.

In order to see the certificate of a Web page, in the page concerned, display the window Security Information, as indicated above. Click on **Open page info** to display more details on its security and the possible risks that you are running. If the active Web page is security certified, **View a Certificate** is displayed. Click on it to view the contents of the certificate.

In order to obtain a certificate:

1. Click on **Communicator, Security Information**. Click on **Certificates** in the left-hand panel (see Figure 9.2).

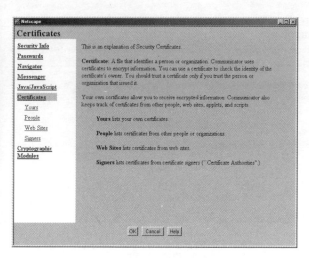

Figure 9.2 Requesting a certificate in Navigator.

2. Click on **Get certificate** (you have to be online). The certi-
   fication page of the Web server of the Netscape company
   is displayed (see Figure 9.3). Select the organisation from
   whom you wish obtain a certificate. It has to offer the following criteria of choice: security, cost and wide accep-
   tance of the certificates.

3. Once you have selected the certificate authority, follow the
   onscreen instructions. You will have to ask for a certificate, give your first name, your surname, your e-mail
   address, your postal address, your country, your date of
   birth and your sex. Opt then for a "shareware" certificate,
   which has the advantage of being free and useable on a
   trial basis for two months. In this way, you will not have
   to rush to a decision. Finish the procedure.

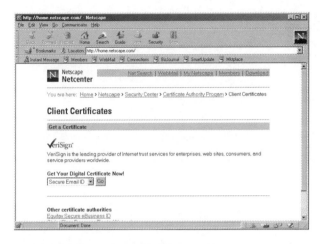

Figure 9.3 Certificates Page at the Netscape site.

Security warning

You can ask Navigator to inform you, with a warning message, if the actions that you are performing represent any danger to the security of your data. Thanks to the on-screen warnings, you remain on top of the situation, and have sole responsibility for the taking of risks, since you have to indicate whether you wish to continue when the warning is displayed.

In order to set up the security warnings, click on **Communicator, Security Information**. In the left-hand panel, click on **Navigator** (see Figure 9.4). Tick the options desired, deselect those that don't suit you, and so on. Click on **OK** when you have finished.

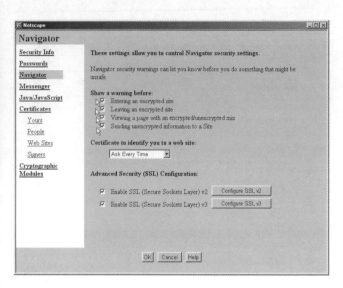

Figure 9.4 Define the settings of the security warnings.

Zones of security

The principle of the security protection in Internet Explorer is not the same as in Navigator, it is more flexible, and it is easier to set up: this is the concept of security zones. The functioning of the security zones is simple: you can classify each Website in one of the security zones suggested, then define a great number options for each of these zones. Subsequently, when you display a Web page, Internet Explorer checks which security zone the page belongs to.

Security zones offered by Internet Explorer:

- **Local Intranet** contains all the addresses which your PC can access locally (Web server or Intranet of your company).

- **Internet** contains all the Web pages that have not yet been assigned to a precise zone.

- **Trusted sites** lets you list all the addresses of Web pages that you trust.
- **Restricted sites** lets you list all the addresses of Web pages that you think might represent a danger to your PC.

In order to enter an address in a security zone:

1. In Internet Explorer, click on **View, Internet Options**. Click on the **Security** tab (see Figure 9.5). Click on the arrow of the Zone option and select the zone desired.

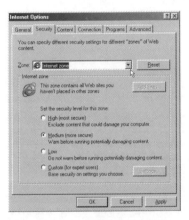

Figure 9.5 Indicate the area in which you wish to add a Web address.

2. Click on **Add sites** (see Figure 9.6). Enter the address desired in the Zone box. Click on Add and click on **OK** to confirm. Click on **OK** in the Options box.

In order to define the level of protection of a security zone, Click on **View, Internet Options**. Click on the Security tab. Click on the arrow of the Zone box and select the zone desired. Tick the level of protection desired. Click on **OK** to confirm.

Figure 9.6 Add a Web address to one of the security zones in Internet Explorer.

ActiveX

ActiveX is a technology that has been developed by Microsoft in competition with Java. The ActiveX controls are binary files, executed directly by the processor; hence, it is almost impossible to monitor exactly what they are doing. A great many Web pages contain ActiveX controls. Given the dangerous nature of these files, it is preferable to disable ActiveX in order to protect your PC.

In order to disable ActiveX in Internet Explorer, click on **View, Internet Options**. Click on the **Security** tab. Click on the arrow of the Zone box and select **Internet**. Under Security level for this zone, select **Custom level** and click on **Settings** (see Figure 9.7). Tick the **Disable** box for the options: Script ActiveX controls marked safe for scripting, Run ActiveX controls and plug-ins, Download signed ActiveX controls, Download unsigned ActiveX controls and Initialize and script ActiveX controls not marked as safe. Click on **OK** to confirm. Click on **OK** in the **Internet Options** box.

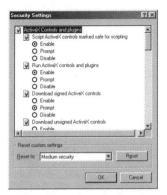

Figure 9.7 Ask Internet Explorer to refuse ActiveX controls.

Java

Java is a programming language created by the Sun company. It will soon be as well known as COBOL was in its time and C++ is nowadays. The characteristic feature of Java is that, once developed, it is executable absolutely everywhere. And it is exactly that which can pose problems: everywhere, which means on your computer too! However, the designers of Java have taken great care over their technology, and its security features work perfectly well. There remains a problem that is not inherent to Java, but which flows from it: since compiler programs are very complex, the programming may contain errors that are dangerous for your system. You may therefore choose to disable the Java applets.

In order to disable Java in Internet Explorer, click on **View**, **Internet Options**. Click on the **Security** tab. Click on the arrow of the Zone box and select **Internet**. Next, click on the **Custom** level of protection and click on **Settings** (see Figure 9.8). In the Java box, tick **Disable**. Click on **OK** to confirm. Click on **OK** in the **Internet Options** box.

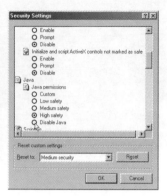

Figure 9.8 Ask Internet Explorer to refuse Java.

In order to disable Java in Navigator, click on **Edit**, **Preferences**. Click on **Advanced** in the left-hand panel (see Figure 9.9). Tick the **Java** box to disable it in the right-hand panel. Click on **OK** to confirm.

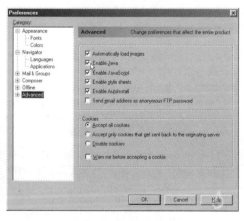

Figure 9.9 Ask Navigator to refuse Java.

JavaScript

JavaScript is a scripting language devised by the Netscape company. Don't be deceived, it has nothing to do with Java. This language offers developers a great many functions for designing interactive Web pages (animation, sound, and so on). These instructions are executed by an interpreting module contained in your browser; hence, JavaScript transmits information on the browser. Certain hackers use this language to plant cookies in your system and read the data. It is therefore preferable to disable JavaScript.

In order to disable JavaScript in Internet Explorer, click on **View, Internet Options**. Click on the **Security** tab. Click on the arrow of the Zone box and select **Internet**. Under Security level for this zone, select **Custom level** and click on **Settings** (see Figure 9.10). In the **Scripting** box, **Scripting of macros...** submenu, tick the **Disable** box. Click on **OK** to confirm. Click on **OK** in the **Internet Options** box.

Figure 9.10 Ask Internet Explorer to refuse JavaScript.

In order to disable JavaScript in Navigator, click on **Edit,
Preferences**. Click on **Advanced** in the left-hand panel (see
Figure 9.11). Tick the **JavaScript** box to disable it in the right-
hand panel. Click on **OK** to confirm.

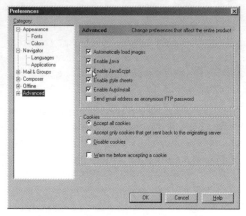

Figure 9.11 Ask Navigator to refuse JavaScript.

Cookies

Cookies are small files that certain Web pages send to your
computer when you are visiting them. Information about
your hard disk is recorded in them and they can then be read
by the Web server that sent them. So a cookie is a tiny spy
that it is preferable to gag. It is true that not all cookies are
motivated by bad intentions, but, as it is hard to discuss mat-
ters with them out in the open, it is preferable to prevent
them being placed on your computer.

To prohibit cookies in Internet Explorer, click on **View,
Internet Options**. Click on the **Advanced** tab (see Figure 9.12).
In the Security zone, Cookies submenu, tick the **Disable** box.
Click on **OK** to confirm. Click on **OK** in the **Internet Options**
box.

Figure 9.12 Ask Internet Explorer to refuse cookies.

To prohibit cookies in Navigator, click on **Edit, Preferences**.
Click on **Advanced** in the left-hand panel (see Figure 9.13).
In the Cookies box, tick the **Disable cookies** box to activate
it in the right-hand panel. Click on **OK** to confirm.

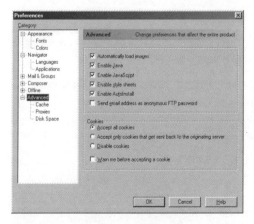

Figure 9.13 Ask Navigator to refuse cookies.

Surveillance of the modem

It isn't always easy to tell if the modem is active or not. Here is a tip for displaying a small icon in the taskbar to indicate whether the modem is active.

To display the modem icon in the taskbar, double-click on **My Computer**. Double-click on **Dial-Up Networking**. Click with the right mouse button on the connection that you use and select **Properties**. Click on **Configure** in the **Connect using** panel. Click on **Options** (see Figure 9.14). Tick the **Display modem status** option to activate it. Click on **OK** to confirm. Click on **OK**.

Figure 9.14 Ask Windows to display an icon symbolising the modem in the taskbar.

Figure 9.15 Modem icon in the taskbar.

■ Protecting payment on the Internet

If you surf regularly on the Internet, you already know that many sites offer products for sale and others, a bit special, are accessible if you pay an entry fee. It is preferable to make your methods of payment secure so as not to take any risk; it would in fact be very unpleasant if someone got hold of your credit card numbers and bought things at your expense.

Microsoft Wallet, which is available in Internet Explorer, lets you make your payments on the Internet secure.

In order to configure Microsoft Wallet:

1. Click on **View, Internet Options**. Click on the **Security** tab. Click on **Payments** (see Figure 9.16).

Figure 9.16 Make payment on the Internet secure.

2. Click on **Add**. Select the type of card desired. Follow the different stages of the Wizard. When you have finished, click on **OK** to confirm. Click on **OK** in the Internet Options box.

■ Protecting e-mail

You have seen in the sixth chapter that you can use many subterfuges and other re-mailers to protect the confidentiality of your messages, encrypt them, and so on. You are going see here how filter your e-mail to avoid, among other things, unwanted messages and advertising material.

Filtering e-mail in Outlook Express

You can create a certain number of rules for filtering your mail, and thus stop being disturbed by intruders.

To create a filter for mail in Outlook Express, click on **Tools**, **Inbox Assistant**. In the dialog box displayed, click on **Add** (see Figure 9.17). Define the filtering options desired. Click on **OK** to confirm.

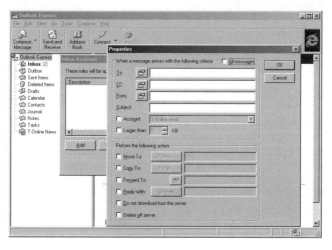

Figure 9.17 Filtering e-mail in Outlook Express.

Filtering e-mail in Messenger

Just as in Outlook Express, you can create filters for optimal handling of your mail.

In order to create a mail filter in Messenger, click on **Edit**, **Message Filters**. Click on **New** (see Figure 9.18). Define the filtering options desired. Click on **OK** to confirm.

Figure 9.18 Filtering e-mail in Messenger.

10

Protecting against viruses

In this chapter, you are going to study everything to do with viruses: the way they work, how they spread, ways to protect yourself, and so on.

■ Viruses

Computer viruses spread in a very simple way, similar to the way biological viruses spread. A virus first needs a vector, that is an action that allows it to infiltrate your system. It has to be via an executable such as a floppy disk or a download, since a virus is a parasitic program that uses the execution of its host program to activate its own functions, namely the reproduction of its code in another program and the execution of the possible functions of the "disease". For this reason, you cannot "catch" a virus by browsing the Web; on the other hand, you begin to take a risk as soon as you begin to download files, freeware, shareware, and to open a program or file liable to contain executable commands, which is notably the case with the macros used in Word or Excel.

The different viruses

It is very hard to say when computer viruses first date from. At the start, the aim was to simulate the process of biological infection on the computer, but the creators quickly proved unable to control the hijacked exploitation of their experiments. Next, some programmers developed their own viruses and released them into the wild, bent on carrying out their mission of destruction.

There are several types of virus; here is a list of them:

■ **Classical Viruses** which infect executable files or install themselves directly on the hard disk. In this case, the virus activates itself each time the application runs, and has the major inconvenience of hiding in the background and breeding in the opened program file.

- **Boot viruses** which infect the boot sector of the hard disk. This means that they are automatically activated when your system is powered up.

- **Cluster viruses** which hide in the unused sectors of the hard disk. They are very dangerous, since they tamper with the information in the file allocation table (FAT).

- **Stealth viruses** which have the characteristic of being invisible and undetectable by an antivirus. They tamper with the system programs and file system in order to wipe out any trace of their presence.

- **Boza virus** which is a virus peculiar to Windows. Released into the wild in 1996, it infects files, then adds a few lines of code to each file. It infects up to three files per folder. At the end of every month, it displays a message to the glory of its designers.

- **Retroviruses** which are the 'nastiest' viruses, since they attack… the antivirus! They then disable it, by deleting files essential to its functioning. Next, it only remains for them to attack the system itself.

Ways for viruses to propagate

There are several possible modes of infection:

- files .exe or .com;
- disk containing a virus that you insert in your disk drive;
- download of files of doubtful origin;
- opening e-mail with files containing viruses attached.

How viruses work

It is estimated that there are 5,000 types of virus currently in circulation, without counting variations on the same theme. They act in many different ways. Some are relatively harmless, others a lot of more frightening and capable of destroying files, or even the whole of the contents of a hard disk. The viral threats are also periodic, and it is important to keep up to date with the nature of the viruses in circulation. But the most worrying is the proliferation of virus attacks. The big increase in the number of computers is not sufficient to explain this increase in the number of infections. In fact, it has become very simple to create one's own viruses. Without any special computer skills, anyone with Internet access can get hold of a virus compiler, or virus libraries, and then have fun infecting everything he can. But what exactly does a virus do? Its first aim: to spread. To this effect, it modifies the executable programs and then contaminates the other programs. But it does not stop there, it acts then in such a way that the programs attacked become unusable, and it destroys some if not all of your data.

Recognising the presence of a virus

You will see in the following pages how you protect against viruses, by installing an antivirus on your computer. That being so, you have to be capable of detecting yourself the possible presence of a virus.

To detect the presence of a virus, keep an eye on your computer, watching out for the following signs:

- A program previously problem-free crashes regularly without reason.

- Your hard disk space is diminishing in an incomprehensible manner.

- The system is temperamental for no apparent reason (no new installation of hardware or software).

- Your files contain strange characters, which you have clearly not entered.

- The computer 'talks to itself'.

- You can no longer change, copy or erase certain files.

- It is impossible to start the computer.

- The peripherals keep malfunctioning (mouse, keyboard, printer, and so on).
- ScanDisk detects many damaged sectors and crossed links.
- The .exe files appear in two places at once.
- The Desktop is changed without any intervention on your part.

■ Macroviruses

The viruses that infect macros are relatively recent. They particularly affect the standard applications such as the ones in Microsoft Office (Word, Excel, and so on). The principle of the macro is simple: a macro is a sub-routine that is used to automate certain tasks. The commands necessary for the macro to work are recorded as part of the document. The viruses that infect macros are command lines resembling normal macros; in this way, they can hide in a text file without you being aware of them, and then spread through your computer. As well as reproducing themselves, extremely quickly, certain of these macroviruses prove to be very dangerous: they are capable of destroying your data automatically.

Recognising the presence of a macrovirus

It is easier to detect a macrovirus than a traditional virus. As soon as you encounter saving problems in an application, you can be sure that there is a macrovirus at the bottom of it. Now, the simplest method is to go and check in the list of the macros of your file to see if there is one that you have not created.

In the list of macros in Word, click on **Tools, Macro, Macros** (see Figure 10.1). Locate the macros named AutoRun or AutoOpen. The macrovirus is frequently inserted into this type of macro.

Figure 10.1 Open the Macros dialog box in Word.

To see the list of macros in Excel, click on **Tools, Macro, Macros**. Locate the macros named AutoRun or AutoOpen. The macrovirus is frequently inserted into this type of macro.

Protection against macroviruses

Of course, you can fight against macroviruses with a traditional antivirus program, as shown in the section 'Ways of protecting against the virus'. However, you can also activate protection against macrovirus offered by Microsoft.

To activate protection against macroviruses, in Word, click on **Tools, Options**. Click on the General tab. Tick the **Macro virus protection** option. Click on **OK** to confirm.

Figure 10.2 Activate the virus protection option in Word.

■ Ways of protecting against viruses

As you have already learned, it is essential to protect yourself against viruses. For this, you must install an antivirus. You are going see in the following pages how to obtain an antivirus, keep it up to date, and so on.

Obtaining an antivirus

There are many antivirus programs available on the market. To obtain one, you have to buy it in a computer shop, then install it on your computer. Here is a list of the main antivirus programs:

- **Norton Antivirus**: very powerful, it is capable of recognising and eliminating thousands of viruses.

- **ThunderByte**: also very powerful, it is very quick and can recognise unknown viruses.

- **VirusScan**: very good program, a bit slow, it was one of the first antiviruses.

- **F-prot**: a good antivirus.

Before buying an antivirus, you can get hold of a demo version from the Websites of the main manufacturers of antivirus programs. Their sites all offer evaluation versions of their products and provide users with the updating necessary for optimal protection of your dear machine. Be aware that, given the way these viruses evolve, it is essential to regularly update the guardian of your hard disk. Here is a list of the Websites of the main antivirus manufacturers:

- **Symantec** for **Norton antivirus** can be found at: **http://www.symantec.com/avcenter/index.html** (see Figure 10.3).

- **ThunderByte** is at: **http://www.thunderbyte.com** (see Figure 10.4).

- **F-Prot** can be found at: **http://www.datafellows.fi/f-prot** (see Figure 10.5).

- **McAfee** for **VirusScan** is at: **http://www.mcafee.com** (see Figure 10.6).

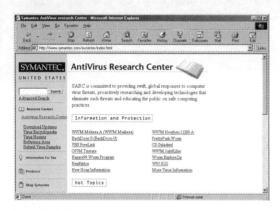

Figure 10.3 The Symantec site.

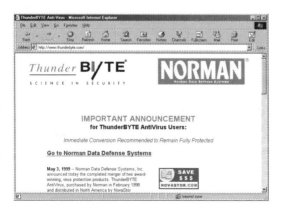

Figure 10.4 The ThunderByte site.

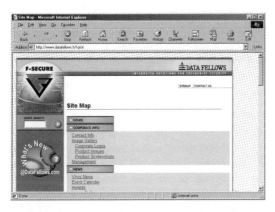

Figure 10.5 The F-prot site.

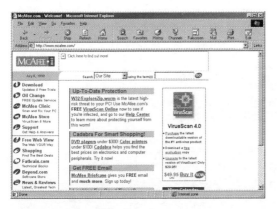

Figure 10.6 The McAfee site.

You will also be able to find a great many protecting and disinfecting tools on the servers of freeware and of shareware. Thanks to its mirror site in the UK, the fastest of these servers appears to be Tucows (**http://tucows.mirror.ac.uk/**).

Viruses are in constant evolution and propagate at the speed of light; hence, your antivirus has to be regularly updated. Visit the site of the manufacturer and download the update. This ensures that you will always be right up to date, and your antivirus program will always be effective.

Installing an antivirus

Once you have obtained your antivirus, you have to install it on your computer. If you have obtained an evaluation version from the manufacturer's Website, all you have to do is to double-click on the installation icon that you have downloaded. On the other hand, if you have bought an antivirus, the procedures are slightly different.

In order to install an antivirus, insert its CD-ROM in the CD-ROM drive, and follow the instructions. You can customise the installation, by stipulating certain options (see Figure 10.7). Once it is done, you have no more worries, since the antivirus will do the work all by itself.

Figure 10.7 Customising the installation of your antivirus.

Hunting viruses

You know that as soon as you download a file, receive a file attached to an e-mail, or are given a floppy disk, it is essential to check it with the antivirus.

To launch the antivirus when, for example, you have downloaded a file:

1. Double-click on the icon of your antivirus in the taskbar (see Figure 10.8) or right-click in Explorer and select **Antivirus**.

Figure 10.8 Icon of your antivirus in the taskbar.

2. Click on **Scan Folder**. Select the folder that you wish to pass to the antivirus (the one containing, for example, the downloaded file) and click on **OK** to confirm (see Figure 10.9).

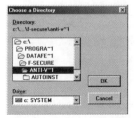

Figure 10.9 Select the folder to pass to the antivirus.

   The antivirus checks the folder. If it discovers a virus, it informs you and then eradicates it. When this happens, it is a good idea to run a check on the whole of your hard disk. The virus can very well "wander" elsewhere than in the folder selected.

3. Click on **OK** when you have finished.

■ Finding out about viruses

The best protection against viruses, in addition to regular updating of your antivirus program, is to keep yourself regularly informed about the new viruses. In this way you will be armed against any virus attack and you will be bang up to date with your information. The first step to take to keep yourself informed is to consult the specialist magazines; they regularly feature information about new viruses. Next, you can gradually visit certain sites that offer masses of information on viruses.

Sites offering information on viruses:

- **Antivirus Online: http://www.av.ibm.com/current** (see Figure 10.10).

Figure 10.10 Online Antivirus Site.

- **Wordinfo: http://www.wordinfo.com/links/macvirus.htm** (see Figure 10.11).

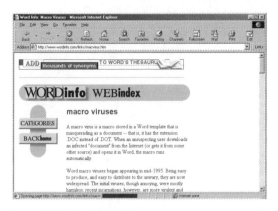

Figure 10.11 Site of Wordinfo.

- Virus information centre:
  http://www.europe.datafellows.com/vir-info/
  (see Figure 10.12).

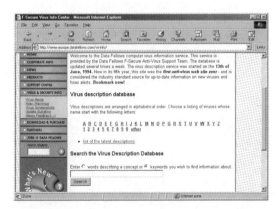

Figure 10.12 Site of Virus information centre.

11
Protecting
the children

■ ■

The truth about the Internet

Protecting children

Protecting yourself... from the children

In the course of this penultimate chapter, you are going study all the procedures for protecting children when they are browsing on the Internet and how to protect yourself... from the children themselves, our dear little angels having a tendency to take a few risks when they use our computer.

■ The truth about the Internet

It has to be admitted, hardly a week passes without the media bashing our ears with some new story about the horrors of the Internet: the breaking up of a paedophile network, pornographic websites, revisionist crackpots, and so on. What is it really like though? First of all, let us consider the problem of what constitutes news. Would Newsnight, for example, have the same viewing figures if they read out news such as: everyone is good-looking, everyone is kind, there has been a very successful summer fair at the local nursery school and nobody is going to die of hunger ever again? The reply unfortunately is 'no'. It's the way of the world; people are hardly interested in good news. Consequently, there is not much chance of a television news programme announcing, along with a large number of reports, that the Internet is brilliant, educational, creative and, in a word, marvellous.

And yet... the Internet is a joy for anyone who wants to get information, develop and educate oneself. It is true that it contains pornographic sites and a few crackpots have found it amusing to publish pages claiming that the concentration camps never existed, that Jews should be exterminated and that Blacks deserve to be bumped off; but there are also many pages offering you a tour round the most beautiful museums in the world, pages on the method for getting the best out of underwater swimming, sites bursting with fabulous and stirring pictures of the World Cup 98, and so on. In short, the Internet is like the world itself: everything is there, the best and the worst, perhaps, the best more often than the worst. That is why it is preferable not to pay any heed to the cynics and not to miss out on the revolution that the Internet offers: access within a few seconds to everything you have always wanted to know about... everything! Moreover, most pornographic sites require a credit card number to authorise entry to their pages, and we may assume that your five year old has not got a Visa card just yet. So don't ban your children from accessing the Internet, since the reality has nothing terrible about it, just the opposite in fact.

■ Protecting children

That is the reality of the Internet. That being so, you can, if you want, restrict access to it. For this you have several tools that you will find out about in what follows. The concept of the filter is both simple and flexible, you can filter according to several criteria: the information provided by the site's webmaster, the lists of addresses and certain specific offers.

Managing access

Internet Explorer puts at your disposal an Access manager to define exactly what you wish to let your children see when they are browsing the Web. It is, in fact, a filter mechanism that relies on the voluntary control of the webmasters of sites. They classify their pages according to certain criteria, and add information about these pages. The criteria are concerned mainly with sex and violence, which are the only real drawbacks to the Internet, as far as children are concerned. With this Access manager, you are going to define exactly the content that you allow your children to view. When you have defined the settings of your Access manager, the browser refers to these settings in the course of browsing and matches the site content against them. If the content corresponds to what you have authorised, the page is displayed; if not, it is blocked, and the page cannot be displayed. The filter criteria used by the Access manager correspond to the RSACi standard.

The RSACi standard is one of the control systems current on the Internet. It offers several evaluation categories :

- Violence;
- Nudity;
- Sex;
- Language.

Configuring the Access manager

You have to define the settings for the Access manager so that it can regulate the browsing of your little dears as closely in accordance with your wishes as possible.

To configure the Access manager:

1. In Internet Explorer, click on **View, Internet Options**. Click on the **Content** tab (see Figure 11.1).

Figure 11.1 The Content tab lets you have access to the Access manager settings.

2. Click on **Activate** in the Access manager window. Enter a password and click on **OK** to confirm (see Figure 11.2).

Figure 11.2 Enter a password.

Click on Settings. Enter the password and click on **OK**. Click on the **General** tab (see Figure 11.3) and deselect the options contained in the **User Options** box.

Figure 11.3 Authorise Internet filtering in advance.

3. Click on the **Control access** tab. Click on the **Language** category, the active standard filter level is displayed (see Figure 11.4). Slide the cursor in the **Control access** option to activate the filtering level desired (see Table 11.1). Click the Nudity category and repeat as before. Continue then in this way for each category. Click on **OK** to confirm when you have finished.

Figure 11.4 Define the filter of the category Language.

Table 11.1 RSACi categories and levels.

Category	Level
Language	0 = inoffensive slang
	1 = very moderate swear words
	3 = obscene gestures
	4 = crude or explicit language
Nudity	0 = none
	1 = revealing clothing
	2 = partial nudity
	3 = frontal nudity
	4 = frontal and provocative nudity
Sex	0 = none
	1 = passionate kissing
	2 = fondling without nudity
	3 = non-explicit fondling
	4 = explicit sexual activity
Violence	0 = none
	1 = fighting
	2 = killing
	3 = bloody killing with shocking details
	4 = gratuitous and cruel violence

Other systems of protection

You can install standards other than RSACi; in fact, there are
other organisations for control of access. For example, the
SafeSurf system, CyberSitter, and so on. In order to find others filtering systems, launch a search on the Internet.
Download the system, then you will be able to install it on
your browser.

In order to install another protection system:

1. Click on **View, Internet Options**. Click on the **Content** tab.
   Click on **Settings** in the Access manager. Enter your password and click on **OK** to confirm.

2. Click on the **Advanced** tab. Click on **Rating systems** (see
   Figure 11.5 and 11.6). Click on **Add**. Double-click on the
   system desired. Click on **OK** to confirm.

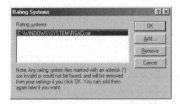

Figure 11.5 The Advanced tab lets you install other filtering systems to
protect children.

Figure 11.6 Activate another filtering system.

Websitter

A few companies have created another control system, which does not require you to define filter settings. They have, in fact, compiled a list of the addresses of sites known to present obscene or questionable content; in this way, the access to these sites is blocked. Moreover, they have introduced another protection system that consists of analysing the text of pages based on a search for key words. If a document contains a forbidden word, the site is automatically rejected. You will find these tools on the Web, by launching a search with the keyword, for example, *websitter* or *supervising children*.

■ Protecting yourself… from the children

You have just studied all the steps to take to protect your children when they are browsing on the Internet. That being so, we should recognise that although it is correct that our dear children must be protected, it is also essential to protect ourselves from them… Thus, it is preferable not to allow access to all the data on your computer, since you would risk having a disaster. Here are a few steps to take to protect your PC from untimely meddling by the children (all the steps to take are described in this book):

- Block the modem when you are not around, since they could surf for hours on the Internet during your absence.

- Create a user profile for the child (see following section).

- Block access to certain programs (see following section).

- Block access to your Explorer; that will avoid them destroying your most important files.

- If they are very young, train them to use a programme such as Paint. In this way they will learn to use the mouse properly, without any risk to your system.

Creating a user profile for the child

You have seen, in the first chapter, that you can create user profiles. These let you define exactly the configuration of the PC, the programs used, and so on, for a given user. The first solution for the children, also the most effective, is to create a personal user profile for each child. Thus, when he starts up the PC, he will select his own user profile and only have access to what you have authorised (programs, Access manager, and so on).

In order to create a user profile for a child:

1. Click on **Start, Settings, Control Panel**. Double-click on **Users**.

2. Click on **New user**. Click on **Next**. Enter in the box the desired name for the user profile (see Figure 11.7). Click on **Next**.

Figure 11.7 Creating a user profile is done with the help of a Wizard.

3. Enter the desired password, then confirm it by entering it again in the box underneath. Click on **Next** (see Figure 11.8).

Figure 11.8 The user profile is accessible by a password that you must not forget.

4. Tick the items whose settings you wish to personalise in the context of the user profile. Click on **Next**. Click on the option **Create new items...** to activate it. Click on **Next** and click on **Finish**. The new user profile is displayed in the list, click on **Close** and close the Control Panel.

Figure 11.9 Defining the items that you wish to personalise in the context of the user profile.

Blocking access to certain programs

Still in the context of protection against the children, it is preferable to block access to certain programs which are vital for your activities. Here is how to do it.

In order to block access to certain programs, after activating the child's user profile, click on **Start, Find, Files or folders** and type *start*. Press Enter. Double-click on **Start** in the list of search results displayed (see Figure 11.10). Click on the application to be deleted and press Delete. Confirm the deletion by clicking on **Yes** in the dialog box which is displayed.

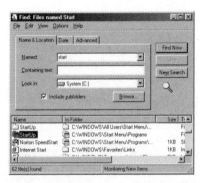

Figure 11.10 Delete a program in the Start group.

From now on, the deleted program will no longer be available to the child.

Apply the procedures of deletion of programs in the child's user profile; otherwise, it is you who will no longer be able to use this program!

Part IV

Passwords

The password is a standard way of protecting a PC, including in the context of sharing the computer. In the course of the chapter in this section of the book, you will find a host of information on the best way of managing passwords, creating them, and so on.

12
Passwords

You are all probably familiar with the classic tale of *Ali Baba and the 40 Thieves*, but just to remind you, the plot goes like this: the thieves' treasure, made up of jewels, gold and other precious metals is hidden in a grotto blocked off by heavy stones. In order to open the entrance to the grotto, the visitor has to say a certain phrase. Of course, only the thieves know it until Ali Baba gets to know it and becomes very rich. Now that you know all the procedures for sharing and protecting your PC, you know that the password is widely used for protecting and sharing data, so you are going to see how, just like the thieves in the film, you can choose words or phrases to restrict access to certain data on your computer. We can therefore, without exaggeration, compare the principle of the password to the 'open, sesame' of the legend.

Imagine the catastrophes that the hacking of your password would cause! Whoever knows your Internet password can surf for hours on the Web, natter on the IRC or participate in news groups, at less cost... to them, but not to you! They can even change the password, which would, if you have access to certain fee-paying services, cost you dear. In fact, even if you are in good faith, try proving to your ISP that you have been the victim of hacking: they will not be interested and will demand to be paid. This is why you must absolutely read this chapter and always follow the advice that you are offered here.

■ Principles of protection by password

It is obvious that the concept of password is the first security procedure to set in place in a computer. It consists of locking up most of your information and preventing unwanted intrusions into your system. You will find here all the types of password that you can create to protect your PC under

Windows 98. You are probably thinking that the notion of passwords is to do with protection, rather than sharing of data. This is incorrect, since one of the most reliable methods to prevent other people who work on the same PC as you having access to your personal or confidential data is to block the access to it by a password. In that way, you will not break out into a cold sweat thinking that Mrs Battleaxe, charming for all that she may be, might find out about the love letter you sent to the switchboard operator, or the application letters you have written with the secret aim of earning more money elsewhere! You have probably heard it said that passwords are not reliable, which is simultaneously both true and false, since, although you can easily avoid the Windows password by simply hitting **Esc** (see Figure 12.1), the fact remains that other passwords, for files for example, are extremely difficult, even impossible, to get round! You will encounter some really difficult ones in the section 'All the passwords'.

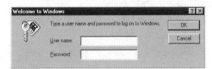

Figure 12.1 Windows password dialog box.

Passwords to avoid

From the various studies done on passwords, it emerges that most of them are unpopular with users, who are often afraid of forgetting them; and, when they use them, they have a tendency to create them without much imagination – which makes them easy to work out. If you choose the date of birth of your only son as a password, there is every chance that your colleague, present at the baptism of the little dear, will work it out! He will be able to access your files, edit them, delete them, and so on, and you will be in a fine mess. In a decidedly more minor key, if the intruder is determined to harm you, he can change your password and block you from access to your own data! We cannot enumerate here all the risks run when your password is cracked; on the other hand, we point out to you, in the section 'Intelligent choice of passwords' a few tips for setting passwords which are difficult to guess, or even impregnable. For the moment, you are going to see, in the following list, the types of password to be avoided like the plague.

Terms, or items, to avoid in the creation of your password:

- **Identity.** It is essential to avoid using anything to do with your identity and that of your close family such as forenames, surnames, and so on.

- **Preferences.** Avoid at all cost making any reference to your various passions and hobbies; for instance, do not choose the make of your car, the eye colour of your sweetheart, your last holiday destination, and so on.

- **Dates.** Forget dates of birth and other dates; it is certain that your colleague will know them.

- **Sentimental references.** Do not tempt fate by choosing to use the name of the nightclub in which you met your partner, or the paradise island where you spent your honeymoon.

Intelligent choice of passwords

You have just seen the items that you should never use to create passwords. Equipped by this advice, you are about to enter your password. Stop! A few further points: avoid terms that are easy to remember with few letters. In fact, let us imagine that short of ideas you have opened the dictionary at the letter T. You decide therefore to choose the word *taxi*. You are confident, since you never use them, do not have a brother in law who is a taxi-driver, and so on. You have simply forgotten that the hackers also have a dictionary!

The first tip is therefore to add at the start and end of a word a letter, a number or a symbol of some sort, so that the word no longer means anything. To go back to our example, add an *a* and a *2*, which gives us *ataxi2*, at least you can say that this password will be very hard to work out! Another method is to use only numbers mixed with special characters. For example, *?458"45=* will be impregnable. The final method is to use a relatively long password, the more characters it contains, the harder to hack it will be. However, be careful not to make it too long, since you might forget it! Ideally, a password of 9 or 10 characters is the optimum.

Golden Rules for protecting passwords

You now have a few passwords to access your user profile, certain folders, files, and so on. To be the owner of a list of passwords is one thing, to have to keep them secret is another. Several rules should be followed to ensure the security of your passwords.

Golden Rules to follow:

- **Do not record passwords.** In the context of the Internet connection, you have to enter a password given to you by the Internet service provider. As soon as you try to connect, a Connection dialog box is displayed (see Figure 12.2), and it lets you record a password. Although it is tedious to have to enter a password each time you connect to the Internet, it is nevertheless preferable not to record it. In fact, if you do, anyone would be able to use your connection and surf for hours on the Web, at your expense!

- **Do not divulge passwords.** A password is the key to all your data, which, of course, is like gold. Just as you would never dream of telling anyone your innermost secrets, never reveal your password to anyone, even to your best friend. Passwords are secret, the fewer people know about them, the more chance they have of remaining secret!

Figure 12.2 Dialog box for the Internet connection. Do not record the password!

- **Do not keep it written down.** Even if your memory is poor, do not write down your various passwords in a file or memo; it is far too risky. If you really cannot manage to remember them, choose them in a way that makes them easy to remember. Here is a tip to help you remember your passwords: make them refer to films or books that you love and will remember easily, and define your password using the first (or second) letters of the title (or the second). For example: Four Weddings and a Funeral gives *fwaaf*; add some characters such as commas, and it's done!

- **Change a password often.** Finally, it is essential to remember to change your password regularly.

All the passwords

Now that you know how to define and protect your passwords in the best possible way, you are going to see everything that Windows offers. For some of them, you are going to see how to create them; for others, we indicate the chapters in which their creation is studied.

The different passwords:

- **BIOS.** The BIOS (*Basic Input Output System*), accessible when you start your computer, contains numerous options for your computer. Protecting it by a password will make it freeze before starting if the person who switched it on does not know the password (see Chapter 7).

- **User Profiles.** These let you define a certain number of setting options for each of the users of the PC and record them in a user profile corresponding to the name of the user (see Figure 12.3). All of these users are allocated one password each in order to let only the owner of each profile access it (see Chapter 1).

Figure 12.3 Dialog box for a user profile.

- **Windows.** It is necessary to be fully aware that the Windows password is not very reliable, since anyone can bypass it by hitting the **Esc** key. However, given that not everyone knows this trick, you will see how to define it in the section 'Creating a password'.

- **Screen saver.** When your computer has not been used for a few minutes, a screen saver is displayed, hiding the Desktop or the file, which you were working on. To get rid of it, all you have to do is to move the mouse; the snag is that anyone can work on the computer, in your user profile, during your absence. In order to prevent intruders, you can block the screen saver with a password (see Figure 12.4).

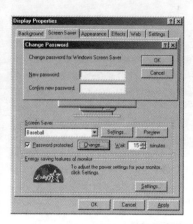

Figure 12.4 Password for the screen saver.

- **Folders and files.** You can create a password to block access to certain folders or files (see Figure 12.5 and Figure 12.6). Consult Chapter 8 for creating this type of password.

Figure 12.5 Password for a file.

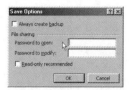

Figure 12.6 Password for a folder.

- **Compression.** You can create a password to block access to your zip files (see Figure 12.7). Thus, no one will be able to decompress your files without your authorisation. Consult Chapter 8 to create this type of password.

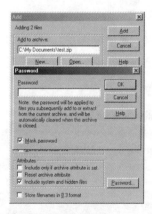

Figure 12.7 Password for compression.

■ Creating the main passwords

In what follows, you are going to see how to create the passwords that have not been studied elsewhere in this book.

Windows password

The password for Windows has to be entered when you start the operating system.

To create a password for Windows:

1. Click on **Start, Settings, Control Panel** (see Figure 12.8).

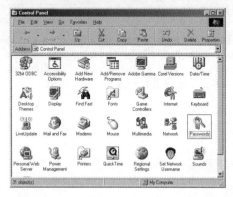

Figure 12.8 The Password icon is accessible from the Control Panel.

2. Double-click on **Passwords** (see Figure 12.9).

Figure 12.9 The dialog box for the Windows password.

3. Click on **Change Windows Password** (see Figure 12.10).

Figure 12.10 Enter your password in both boxes.

4. Press **Tab** to move directly into the password window. Enter your password in both boxes, and confirm by clicking on **OK**. Click again on **OK**. Close the Control Panel.

Password for the screen saver

You are going see how to block the screen saver in order to prevent someone from using your computer in your absence.

To create the password for the screen saver:

1. Click with the right mouse button on the Desktop. Select **Properties**.

2. Click on the **Screen saver** tab (see Figure 12.11).

Figure 12.11 The Screen saver has to be activated to define its password.

3. In the **Screen Saver** tab, click on the arrow and choose a screen saver. Then click the **Password protected** box to activate it. Click on **Change** (see Figure 12.12).

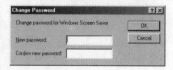

Figure 12.12 Enter your password twice.

4. Click on **OK** to confirm.

■ Organising passwords

You have seen in the previous chapters how to create the various passwords for the system, files, and so on. Now we shall learn how to change or delete it. We return to the example of the ones you have just created; these steps are the same for the other passwords.

Managing the password for Windows

As we showed you earlier in this chapter, it is essential to change passwords regularly. You will find out below how to proceed. Moreover, if you are unhappy with this password, you can of course delete it.

In order to change the password for Windows, you have to repeat the procedures for creating it in the **Change Windows Password** dialog box: entering the old password in the **Old password** box, then entering the new password in the **New password** box, and finally confirming the password by entering it in the **Confirm new password** box. Then click on **OK** to confirm.

In order to delete the Windows password, you have to repeat the procedures for changing it as explained above without entering anything in the New Password box. Then click on **OK** to confirm.

Managing the screen saver password

At the risk of repeating ourselves: you must change your password regularly. Here is how to change the screen saver password. Next, you will see how to delete it, if need be.

In order to change the password for the screen saver, you have to open the Properties dialog box by clicking with the right mouse button on the Desktop and by selecting **Properties**. Then click on the **Screen saver** tab. Click on **Change**. Enter the new password in both boxes and then click on **OK** to confirm. Click again on **OK**.

To delete the password for the screen saver, open the Properties dialog box by clicking with the right mouse button anywhere on the Desktop and select **Properties** in the context menu. Then click on the **Screen saver** tab. Click on **Password protected** to disable it. Click on **OK** to confirm.

Index

....